101

PLACES

NOT

TO SEE

before you die

Catherine Price

HARPER

NEW YORK · LONDON · TORONTO · SYDNEY

HARPER

HarperCollins books may be purchased for educational, business, or sales
promotional use. For information, please write: Special Markets Department,
HarperCollins Publishers, 10 East 53rd Street, New York, NY 10022.

FIRST EDITION

Designed by Daniel Lagin

Library of Congress Cataloging-in-Publication Data
Price, Catherine, 1978–
    101 places not to see before you die/by Catherine Price.—1st ed.
        p. cm.
    Summary: "A spirited, ingenious, tongue-in-cheek guide to some of the least
appealing destinations and experiences in the world"—Provided by publisher.
    Includes index.
    ISBN 978-0-06-178776-8
    1. sc22   2010004502

10 11 12 13 14   ID/RRD   10 9 8 7 6

101

PLACES

NOT

TO SEE

before you die

For my grandmother

✦ CONTENTS ✦

✦ INTRODUCTION ✦

There are a lot of things I need to do before I die.

Or at least that's what my local bookstore is telling me. Every time I visit, I'm faced with a shelf's worth of guides listing things to accomplish, from *100 Places to See in Your Lifetime* to *101 Things to Do Before You're Old and Boring*. I appreciate the idea behind Patricia Schultz's *1,000 Places to See Before You Die*, the inspiration for this genre of books, but its offspring stresses me out.

There are lists of jazz albums I need to listen to, foods I must taste, paintings I have to see, walks I'm required to take—my own father has a book of 1,001 gardens I can't die without visiting. How am I supposed to conquer 1,001 movies while simultaneously reading 1,001 books and traveling to 1,001 historic sites—not to mention making it to the 500 places I must see before they disappear? By the time I found a copy of *101 Places to Have Sex Before You Die*, I was tempted to swear off travel books, grab a selection of the 1,001 beers I have to drink, and head to one of the 1,001 spots where I'm supposed to escape.

I am a person who routinely writes lists of things I've already done, just to make myself feel more accomplished. Like many people, I already spend too much time coming up with arbitrary things I "should" be doing, keeping myself so busy that it's hard to separate one moment from the next. The last thing I need to read is a book that pits my desire for adventure against the time pressure of mortality—especially in the form of 1,001 places I'm supposed to play golf.

So I decided to create an antidote: a list of places and experiences that you don't need to worry about missing out on. I called upon travel-loving friends, family members, and, in some cases, complete strangers to tell me about overhyped tourist sites, boring museums, stupid historical attractions, and circumstances that can make even worthwhile destinations miserable.

Some entries on the list are unquestionably unappealing, like a field strewn with decomposing bodies or fan hours at the Las Vegas porn convention. Some depend on context—Pamplona's a very different city from the perspective of a bull. Some are just good stories, albeit ones that are more fun to read about than to experience firsthand.

As I gathered suggestions, I came across a characteristic common among frequent travelers: a reluctance to define anything as bad. "I have a soft spot for underdog places and a perverse need to find even the worse stuff a source of delight and titillation," wrote one friend about her inability to hate on Uzbekistan or, for that matter, Detroit. She's right, of course—the worse something is in the moment, the better the story when you get home. So for those people who look at a warehouse full of rotting human sewage and see an interesting way to spend an afternoon, I also included some places that would be impossible to visit even if you were intent on finding the bright side in everything, like the Yucatán Peninsula sixty-five million years ago or the bottom of the Kola Superdeep Borehole. It might seem pointless to say that you shouldn't go to a place like Io, Jupiter's least hospitable moon, but look at it this way: when someone publishes *1,001 Places in Space to See Before You Die*, the pressure will be off.

No matter what type of traveler you are, I invite you to take a break from your other to-do lists and spend a moment being grateful for some of the things you're *not* doing. Then, when you're ready to hit the road, leave behind your list of *1,001 Places You Must Pee** and give yourself a chance to come up with some experiences of your own. Travel should be an adventure, not an assignment, and if you spend your vacations armed with too many checklists, you're missing the point of leaving home.

---

* Not kidding.

101

PLACES

NOT

TO SEE

before you die

1   THE TESTICLE FESTIVAL

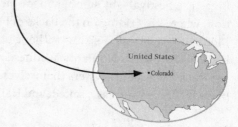

Forget apple pie. Few foods are as uniquely American as the Rocky Mountain oyster, a euphemism that refers not to a high-altitude mollusk but to the testicles of a bull. Also known as cowboy caviar and Montana tendergroin, these balls can be boiled, sautéed, or even eaten raw, but they're usually treated more like chicken—breaded and deep-fried.

There are also few things more American than eating competitions, so it should come as no surprise that each summer offers opportunities to prove your manhood by stuffing your face with gonads. I appreciate the pun of the Nuts About Rocky Mountain Oysters competition that occurs annually in Loveland, Colorado. But the award for Best in Show goes to the Testicle Festival, held each year at the Rock Creek Lodge near Missoula, Montana. Started in 1982, it is America's premier venue to chow down on balls.

When the festival first began, it drew about three hundred people. But these days the crowd has grown to fifteen thousand, and the debauchery has expanded to a weekend full of wet T-shirts, impromptu nudity, and an Indy 500–inspired race called the "Undie 500"—all natural evolutions of an event whose tagline is "Come Have a Ball." Try your hand at Bullshit Bingo, a larger-than-life—and quite literal—game of chance where every time a bull defecates on a giant bingo card, someone wins $100. Or support the event's alternate title—the Breasticle Festival—by signing up for the Biker Ball-Biting Competition, where girls riding on the backs of Harleys race to snag a Rocky Mountain oyster off a string without using their hands. There are belly shots. There's No Panty Wednesday. And, of course, there are the Rocky Mountain oysters themselves—more than fifty thousand pounds of them—greasy, salted, and USDA-approved.

2

AN UNDERPASS IN CONNAUGHT CIRCLE, NEW DELHI, AT THE MOMENT WHEN SOMEONE PUTS A TURD ON YOUR SHOE

New Delhi ★

India

Imagine this scene: you're walking through an underpass in Connaught Circle, a mess of traffic where twelve of New Delhi's roads converge, and all of a sudden a voice calls out of the crowd.

"Excuse me, friend," it says. "You've got feces on your shoe."

Several weeks in India have made you realize that when people yell at you on the street, it's usually best to ignore them. So at first you pay no attention. But something in this man's voice is different, believable. He repeats himself, and you slowly lower your eyes.

And there it is: a flattened turd sitting on the top of your shoe.

Your first reaction is disbelief—you've had shit on the *bottom* of your shoe, sure. But the top? How can this be? There aren't any birds around, or monkeys. Disgusted, you lean down to inspect it. Still moist and glistening, it gives off a familiar fecal smell.

You consider throwing up, but before your gag reflex can kick in, a voice pipes up. "Don't worry, I will clean it for you." It is your new friend, who now is standing next to you with a shoe-shining kit. Well, will you look at that! Here you are, caught in the one moment in your life where you need an emergency shoe cleaning, and this kind man pops out of nowhere to help you. What are the odds?

Before you have a moment to actually calculate the odds of this happening coincidentally, the man has escorted you off to the side of the passageway where, with a flourish, he rids your shoe of the offending turd. Then, as you reach into your wallet for a tip, he announces the price for a shit-shine special—and it's more than most New Delhi residents earn in a week.

If you think about it, the scam is brilliant. The service has already been rendered, and besides, who wants to walk around with a turd perched on his shoe?

So you pay him—not his asking price, but still enough to make it worth his while to continue smearing poop on the footwear of passersby. If you're a victim, feel free to get pissed off. But at least the shit scheme isn't as bad as the loogie-on-your-shoulder trick. In that one, you don't even have the chance to give a tip—someone smears a wad of spit on your jacket while a second guy steals your wallet.

3 EURO DISNEY

I've never liked Disney World. As a child who was terrified of mimes, Santa Claus, and any larger-than-life stuffed animal, I hated the giant mice that roamed the streets of the Magic Kingdom, holding children hostage until their parents took a photograph. Huge, unblinking eyes; garish smiles; swollen, cartoon hands—this was the stuff of nightmares. When my parents brought me to a special event called "Breakfast with the Characters," I took one look at Pinocchio and dove under the table.

So perhaps I was biased against Euro Disney from the start. But really, who wasn't? Opened in 1992, it was an attempt to bring Mickey Mouse to Europeans—an audience that tends to be skeptical of American culture to begin with, especially when it tries to steal the hearts and minds of its children. Convinced that parental disapproval was no match for their offspring's love of *The Little Mermaid*, Disney pushed forward with its plans and eventually settled on a spot in the rural town of Marne-la-Vallée. An easy train ride from Paris, the location was estimated to be less than a four-hour drive for sixty-eight million people.

Controversy soon followed. Assuming that there must be a direct connection between Euro Disney and the U.S. government, French farmers blockaded its entrance with their tractors to protest European and American agricultural policies. A Parisian stage director named Ariane Mnouchkine called Euro Disney a "cultural Chernobyl," and while she quickly moved on to making other exaggerated comparisons to nuclear disasters ("Television seems to me to be a much more menacing cultural Chernobyl," she told the *New York Times* in July 1993), the classification stuck.

And then there were tactical errors: Euro Disney opened, for example, in the middle of a European recession. It offended would-be workers with a strict dress code forbidding long nails and requiring "appropriate undergarments" for women, which prompts the question of why a Disney employee would be showing her undergarments to begin with. As a primarily outdoor attraction, it didn't take into account the fact that France, unlike Florida and Southern California, actually has a winter. The restaurants in the park also didn't serve

alcohol, a policy that didn't go over well with Europeans used to enjoying a glass of wine with lunch. By July 1993—a little over a year after the park opened—Euro Disney had debts of about $3.7 billion.

But despite the challenges of translating Americana into every European language (in Italian, Cattleman's Chili is *Pepperoncino alla Cowboy*) Euro Disney kept fighting. The park posted its first profits in 1995 and has done so intermittently since then. Scarred by the negative connotations of "Euro Disney," it also changed its name to "Disneyland Paris." Former Disney CEO Michael Eisner says this title was chosen to identify the park with "one of the most romantic and exciting cities in the world," but this seems like an odd association—the place is so quintessentially American that it has an Aerosmith-themed roller coaster.

4 IBIZA ON A FAMILY VACATION

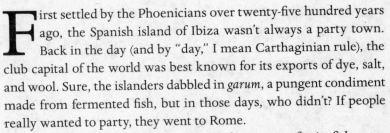

First settled by the Phoenicians over twenty-five hundred years ago, the Spanish island of Ibiza wasn't always a party town. Back in the day (and by "day," I mean Carthaginian rule), the club capital of the world was best known for its exports of dye, salt, and wool. Sure, the islanders dabbled in *garum*, a pungent condiment made from fermented fish, but in those days, who didn't? If people really wanted to party, they went to Rome.

Times have changed. Today Ibiza is known not for its fish sauce but for clubbing, promiscuity, and an abundance of illicit drugs. A favorite holiday destination for the world's horniest youth, Ibiza's flesh-baring clientele and encouragement of casual sex have earned it the nickname "Gomorrah of the Med."

Until recently, the government was happy to bear the responsibility for a few extra STDs in exchange for the purchasing power of thousands of hormonally fueled visitors. But then, after some thirty years of tolerance, it closed several prominent clubs for part of the 2007 season, citing evidence of illegal drug use. Among its arguments: one of the clubs had telephone booths that contained traces of cocaine, snorting tubes, bloody tissues, and, incidentally, no phones. But with possible sexual partners on all sides anyway, who would have needed to place a call? When the clubs eventually reopened, it was with limitations: the government banned clubs from operating past 6 in the morning (they used to stay open all day), and is now trying to actively push Ibiza as a family vacation destination.

Considering that Ibiza has thousands of years' worth of archaeo-logical remains—not to mention several UNESCO World Heritage Sites—this isn't entirely preposterous. And yet, I still find it difficult to imagine a family vacation in the midst of an Ibizan summer. Where would you take the kids first? Amnesia, a giant club famous for its foam parties? Or Es Paradis, where every night thousands of ample-bosomed girls wearing white T-shirts are sprayed with a fire hose?

Pick your poison, but don't let the kids leave Ibiza without an outing to Privilege, the world's largest club. With a capacity for ten thousand people, its airplane hangar–size space offers something for everyone: you and your spouse can gyrate with thousands of sweaty partiers next to the indoor pool while a stranger teaches your five-year-old how to spell "ecstasy" and your teenager samples ketamine in the bathroom. Just make sure that if your family gets separated, no one tries to find a phone.

5 THE BEIJING MUSEUM OF TAP WATER

hen you're dealing with two languages as different as Chinese and English, it's inevitable that some things get lost in translation. Handicapped bathrooms are occasionally referred to as "Deformed Man End Places." In Dongda, the proctology center used to be known as the Hospital for Anus and Intestine Disease. Occasionally, a place receives a title that's both bizarre-sounding *and* mundane. Case in point: the Beijing Museum of Tap Water.

The history of Beijing's tap water dates back to 1908, when the Empress Dowager Cixi supported a plan to build a water system for Beijing. The museum, however, is a recent addition—it's the result of a 2001 edict requiring that 150 new museums open in Beijing by 2008. As any curator can attest, 150 is an awful lot of new museums to build in seven years. The result: in addition to tap water, Beijing also now has museums devoted to honeybees, red sandalwood, and goldfish.

Housed in a former pump house, the tap water museum starts with the founding of Beijing's first water company, the Jingshi Tap Water Co., and features artifacts like vintage water coupons and a stethoscope used to listen for water leaks. It also boasts not just 130 "real objects," but 110 pictures, 40 models, and a miniature tap water filtration system. Step aside, Forbidden City.

The weirdest thing about the museum, though, is that the substance it's meant to commemorate—clean tap water in Beijing—doesn't actually exist. Yes, in 2007 Beijing was the first Chinese city whose water officially passed a test for 106 contaminants. But thanks to the condition of the pipes transporting it from stations to people's taps, it's still unsafe to drink.

6 A BATHTUB FILLED WITH BEER

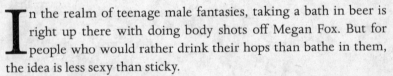

Czech Republic

In the realm of teenage male fantasies, taking a bath in beer is right up there with doing body shots off Megan Fox. But for people who would rather drink their hops than bathe in them, the idea is less sexy than sticky.

If you fall into the latter camp, skip the Chodovar brewery in the Czech Republic. Billed as "Your beer wellness land," it offers hops-crazed visitors the chance to soak their cares away in bathtubs full of their favorite beverage. Complete with warm mineral water and a "distinct beer foam of a caramel color," the brewery's special dark bathing beer contains active beer yeast, hops, and a mixture of crushed herbs. But the fun doesn't end with the bath: afterward, guests are led to a relaxation area where they are wrapped in a blanket in a dim room with pleasant music and given one of several complimentary drinks.

"The procedures have curative effects on the complexion and hair, relieve muscle tension, warm up joints, and support immune system of the organism," says Dr. Roman Vokaty, the spa's official balneologist, in response to the obvious question of why a beer bath is a good idea. One could argue that the combination of a post-bath massage and the bottles of Chodovar's lager consumed *while* the organism soaks in the tub might have just as much, if not more, of an impact on the organism's well-being than the beer's carbon dioxide and ale yeasts. But then, I'm not a balneologist.

If you like the idea of wasting a perfectly good drink, check out some of Europe's other beer spas: Starkenberg in Austria, for example, has been known to fill an entire swimming pool with Pilsner, and the Landhotel Moorhof in Franking, Austria, offers a brewski facial made from ground hops, malt, honey, and cream cheese. According to one survivor, it "smells remarkably like breakfast."

7 AN OVERNIGHT TRAIN IN CHINA ON THE FIRST DAY OF YOUR FIRST PERIOD

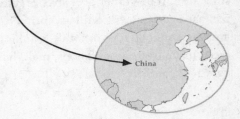

China

June 16, 1991, was Father's Day. It was also the day I got my period for the first time, and it occurred right in the middle of a family vacation to China—a three-week self-guided journey with my parents and my mom's seventy-year-old friend, Betty.

I was mortified. To make things worse, the hotel we were in didn't have sanitary supplies, and in China at the time it was difficult to find a store opened to foreigners at all, let alone one with Western toiletries. Had we been in America, the next step would have been for us to go to a drugstore together where I, too embarrassed to pick out sanitary products myself, would inspect the toothbrush display as my mother yelled questions from the next row over like "Scented or non-scented?" and "Do you want wings?" Instead, my mother convinced me to allow her to tell Betty; the two conferred in hushed tones, and when back in my room, Betty rummaged through her toiletry bag and presented me with a Depends.

Wearing an adult diaper as a twelve-year-old added insult to the injury of menstruation, and our itinerary only made things worse.

Presumably if we'd been sticking around at our hotel, we would have been able to find maxi-pads somewhere in the city before Betty's supplies ran out. However, my parents, eager for an authentic, self-guided China experience, had arranged for us to get on a train to a city twenty-three hours away. No sooner had we left for the station than my body, unsatisfied with the humor of me simply menstruating on a Chinese train, broke out in hives. My mother gave me two extra-strength Benadryl. I stumbled to the train platform with my parents and woke up three hours later on an upper bunk in a moving train, in a car with vomit stains on the carpet and circles at the end of each bed where people's heads had wiped away the dirt. My parents and Betty were giggling on the bunks below me as they played bridge and drank "tea" they'd brewed from water and Johnny Walker Black. I needed to use the bathroom.

I slid off the top bunk and unlatched the door to our cabin to find the toilet, but my mother stopped me before I could leave.

"It's clogged," she said. "Betty and I tried to use it, and it smells so bad, we almost threw up."

"What am I supposed to do?"

"Do what we did," said my mother, which was greeted by tipsy laughter from Betty and my father. "Pee in this."

My mother then handed me a Ziploc bag.

What bothered me about this was not so much the fact that my mother was telling me to urinate into a freezer bag, but rather, how I could do so with my father in the room. Holding the empty bag, I glared at my mother, glanced at my father, and then glared at her again until she realized what I was trying to communicate.

"Richard, go out in the hall. Catherine needs some privacy."

With my mother and Betty playing cards in front of me, I squatted down, pulled down my pants, pushed aside my diaper, and peed into the bag, trying my best to keep my balance on my heels as the train rocked back and forth.

"I don't want it," my mother said when I tried to hand it to her. "Give it to your father." I slid the door open and found him standing in the hallway watching rice paddies out the window. A childhood polyps operation gone awry left him with no sense of smell, so he took the bag when I offered it and carried it down the hall to the bathroom. He stuffed the bag down the toilet with a hanger, it burst upon the tracks, and he returned to our cabin to finish his tea.

When we arrived at our hotel in Beijing the next day, my family's first destination was the Summer Palace. My first destination was the bathroom, a squat building a short, urine-scented walk away from the park entrance. Inside, a long row of waist-high, doorless stalls subdivided a porcelain trough pitched slightly toward one end of the room, over which women squatted on their heels, bottoms bared to the world. Some read magazines; most held tissues clamped to their noses to keep out the stench. Driven by the pressure of my bladder and the presence of my Depends, I ignored the smell and forged ahead toward the end of the room, picking the last stall so that I would be exposed to the fewest number of people possible. I glanced around to see if anyone was watching and yanked my pants to my knees, realizing only when I looked down that my stall was downstream from the other seven.

The second thing I noticed was that my period had stopped—apparently it had decided that two and a half days was sufficient for a first-time visit. This filled me with joy until I realized that, now that I had begun to ovulate, it would return once a month for the rest of my child-bearing years. When I looked up to the ceiling in a "Why, God?" moment, my eyes were stopped halfway by a third realization: despite my attempts at seclusion, the other women in the room had seen me enter. Curious about what a Caucasian twelve-year-old would look like while urinating, several had walked up to where I was squatting and were standing next to my stall, giggling behind their tissues as they stared at my naked backside. I felt self-conscious enough simply being an American in China, but being watched in a bathroom while wearing a diaper was as embarrassing as going bra shopping with my father. I pulled my pants up and they scattered back to their places in line as I pushed past them, ashamed. If this was what it meant to be a woman, I wanted to go home.

Postscript: I returned to China in the summer of 2002 and am happy to report that train travel has remarkably improved. Unfortunately, however, my bottom is still considered a tourist attraction—when my friend and I visited a public squat toilet, we looked up to find a group of women taking photographs.

GRANDPA AND GRANDMA, KOH SAMUI, THAILAND

If I suggested that you visit the Grandpa and Grandma Rocks on Thailand's Lamai Beach, what would you expect to see? The silhouettes of two aged lovers? A piece of granite resembling wrinkled hands intertwined? No and no. Grandma and Grandpa are rock formations that look like genitalia.

When I first heard about these rocks—referred to locally as Hin Ta and Hin Yai—I thought that seeing genitalia in the rocks might require effort, like how it takes a certain degree of creativity to find Jesus in your toast. But these grandparents aren't subtle. Granddad is clearly a large, erect penis. And Grandma has spread her legs open to the sea, positioned so that she's caressed by every wave that hits the shore.

When you see the rocks, you will probably wonder whether people in Thailand have a very different relationship with their grandparents from what we have in America. Perhaps, but in this particular case, the nickname comes from a legend—Ta Kreng and Yai Riem, an elderly couple, were on their way to try to procure a bride for their grandson from a family to the north when their boat got caught in a storm. They drowned. And then, as so often befalls seafaring grandparents, they were turned into rocks representing their respective naughty bits.

These days, it's probably best not to bother visiting unless you enjoy fighting your way through street vendors selling phallic souvenir T-shirts just so that you get a picture of yourself perched on Grandma's thigh. The beach isn't particularly good for swimming, and you'll be surrounded by people who decided that, of the many attractions Thailand has to offer, all they really wanted to see was a granite penis.

Grandpa

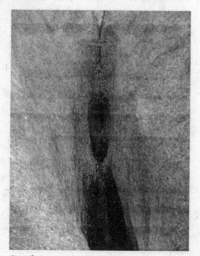

Grandma

THE WINCHESTER
MYSTERY HOUSE

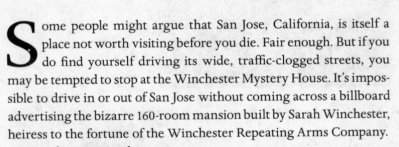

United States

•San Jose

Some people might argue that San Jose, California, is itself a place not worth visiting before you die. Fair enough. But if you do find yourself driving its wide, traffic-clogged streets, you may be tempted to stop at the Winchester Mystery House. It's impossible to drive in or out of San Jose without coming across a billboard advertising the bizarre 160-room mansion built by Sarah Winchester, heiress to the fortune of the Winchester Repeating Arms Company.

But please, resist the urge.

The story of the Winchester Mystery House—or, rather, the legend—is as follows: after her infant daughter and husband passed away, Sarah Winchester visited a psychic who told her that her loved ones' deaths were caused by the souls of the people who had been killed by the Winchester repeating rifle (tagline: "The Gun That Won the West"). If she didn't take drastic action, said the psychic, Sarah Winchester could be next. The psychic supposedly told her that the only way to appease the angry spirits was to go west and build a house—not too difficult a task for a woman who had an income of about $1,000 a day in the late 1800s. But there was one catch: the house could never be completed. If construction ever stopped, the spirits would seek their revenge once more.

And so Sarah Winchester moved from Connecticut to San Jose, bought an unfinished eight-room farmhouse, and started construction. She hired shifts of men to work around the clock, seven days a week, 365 days a year. From the day she began until her death thirty-eight years later, the workers never stopped. Every evening, legend has it, Sarah Winchester would retreat to a special séance room in the middle of the house to commune with lost souls and, while she was at it, figure out the next day's construction plans.

The result is a sprawling mansion that gives a sense of what happens when a multimillion-dollar fortune and a belief in the paranormal are combined in a woman with no architectural training. There are stairs that lead to the ceiling, chimneys that stop a foot and a half short of the roof, cabinets that are actually passageways, and a second-story "door to nowhere" that opens fifteen feet above the ground outside. Throughout the house are touches of grandeur—hand-inlayed floors, Tiffany glass windows—and bizarre architectural elements, like custom-designed window panes in the shape of spider webs and a preoccupation with the number thirteen.

The house has been open to the public, in one form or another, since soon after Winchester's death in 1922. But unfortunately for anyone intrigued by her story, its legend is more interesting than the tour itself. Part of the problem is that Winchester left all of her furniture, household goods, pictures, and other artifacts to her niece, the alliterative Mrs. Marian Merriman Marriott, who wasted no time in clearing out the house and selling them off. This was no doubt profitable for Mrs. M, but it means that aside from a few rooms that have been refurnished with period-appropriate decor, the gigantic house is empty. What's more, despite the legend of the house—the séances, the spirits, the psychic—no one really knows for certain *why* Sarah Winchester built her house the way she did. Maybe the story is true; maybe she was just participating in an early-twentieth-century version of *Extreme Home Makeover*. Or maybe she was just bat-shit crazy.

Regardless, like all good tourist traps, the opportunities to spend money at the Winchester House don't end with the tour. In addition to an arcade offering 1980s video games, there's an antique products museum featuring Winchester flashlights, Winchester roller skates, and Winchester wrenches, and a display titled WINCHESTER HOUSE IMMORTALIZED IN GINGERBREAD. The nearby gift shop is a warehouse-size collection of Winchester House shot glasses, tote bags, T-shirts, and specialty wine, all sharing shelf space with butterfly-shaped wind chimes, novelty dishtowels, and magnets announcing that "STRESSED" IS "DESSERTS" SPELLED BACKWARDS.

The effect of all this—the gift shop, the mile-long tour through endless empty rooms, the near total lack of concrete facts—is to leave you feeling as if you'd just binged on McDonald's: full, and yet, surprisingly empty. In fact, the only justification for the house's popularity as a tourist attraction is its size—whereas usually one would balk at the prospect of paying $26 to tour a crazy lady's empty home ($5 more if you want to see the plumbing system), the Winchester House is so large that with some creative math, it's almost justifiable: each of its 110 rooms costs less than 25 cents to see.

But still, one question remains: who signs up for the annual pass?

Nota bene: The Winchester Mystery House is not to be confused with the pirate-themed haunted house that opens in Fremont, California, every Halloween. That is totally different—though, incidentally, also not worth seeing.

✕✕✕✕ A.J. JACOBS ✕✕✕✕

The Worst Places in the Encyclopedia

Paris in 1871

During the famous Siege of Paris, food was hard to come by. The residents resorted to "rat paté." Or, if they were lucky and had connections, they got to eat the giraffes and elephants from the Paris zoo. Not a place you want to visit unless you have an extremely adventurous palate.

The Emperor's Court in China, Twelfth Century

It's hard to pick the most evil ruler in the encyclopedia, but among the top ten was probably Emperor Chou. To please his concubine, Chou built a lake of wine and forced naked men and women to chase one another around it. Also, he strung the forest with human flesh.

The Eighth Circle of Hell

In Dante's book *The Divine Comedy*, the ninth circle of hell is traditionally considered the worst. In this circle, betrayers are stuck in a frozen lake for eternity, their tears making blocks of ice on their eyes. But personally, I think the eighth circle sounds worse. This one has a river of human excrement that submerges flatterers. To me, ice sounds pretty good next to that.

The North End of Boston on January 15, 1919

This may be a stretch for this list, but I try to mention the Great Molasses Flood in everything I write. And it really was a bad place to be. It occurred when a giant molasses storage tank exploded and sent a fifteen-foot wave of molasses through the streets of Boston. Twenty-one people were drowned in the sticky stuff. Trains were lifted off their tracks and horses were submerged in the strangest and sweetest disaster in history.

A. J. JACOBS is the author of *The Know-It-All: One Man's Humble Quest to Become the Smartest Person in the World.*

XXXX

10 HELL

Regardless of which circle you deem the worst, I think we can all agree that hell is not a great place to visit. Whether you choose to stop by the Greek and Roman Tartarus or the horrible O le nu'u-o-nonoa of Samoan mythology, you're likely to be treated to some blend of fire, ice, and demons. Oh, and pain. Lots and lots of pain.

The many variations of hell are a testament to humans' ability to invent unusual methods of torture. But when it comes to specifics, you have to hand it to Zoroastrianism. Its version of hell includes precise punishments for everything from approaching fire or water when you're menstruating to unlawfully slaughtering a sheep.

If I had to pick a hell to visit, I'd probably go with the one in Michigan. Complete with a fictional nonaccredited college that offers "signed, sealed and singed diplomas," Hell, Michigan, is a small town about twenty-five miles by car northwest of Ann Arbor that focuses more on puns than on punishments. Eager to capitalize on its name, the town has a part-time post office (for people who get their thrills through postmarks) and a tagline—"A little town on its way up." And, for couples whose definition of romance includes fire and brimstone, Hell also has a wedding chapel.

11 A *BUZKASHI* MATCH

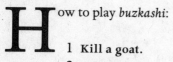

Afghanistan

How to play *buzkashi*:

1 Kill a goat.
2 Behead it.*
3 Disembowel it.
4 Soak it in cold water for twenty-four hours to toughen it up.
5 Give it to crazed men on horseback to play a violent, gruesome game.
6 Barbecue!

An Afghani tradition, *buzkashi* is an animal-rights advocate's nightmare: a sport in which three teams of horsemen compete to score goals with the body of a dead, headless goat.

But that makes it sound too easy. In order to score goals, horsemen first have to grab the goat and carry the seventy-pound carcass around a small post. Then they gallop seventy-five yards down the

---

* Steps 2 and 3 may be combined.

field and hurl the goat into a small chalk circle. All this happens while they and their horses are being beaten, whipped, punched, and otherwise attacked by the other players, who can do anything, save tripping a horse, to prevent the other teams from scoring. Few games end without a horse trampling at least one rider or, for that matter, a spectator—*buzkashi* fields don't have boundaries.

Dexter Filkins, a war correspondent for the *New York Times*, witnessed a near disaster when a player rode his horse directly into the crowd. "Spectators scattered and screamed as the horses thundered close," he wrote. "The referee reached for his Kalashnikov, then thought better of it.

' "Run!' a boy squealed. 'Ha! Ha! Ha! Run!' "

When the game ends—which can take days, since there's no official time limit or set number of goals—the winning team gathers for the traditional end of the game: barbecuing the goat. *Buzkashi* means goat-pulling, after all, and according to a hungry old man interviewed by Filkins, "All that pulling and stretching makes it very tender."

Note the goat

12 YOUR BOSS'S BEDROOM

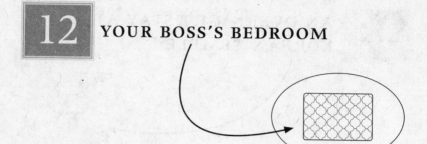

This does not count as corporate team building.

13 AN OVERNIGHT STAY AT A KOREAN TEMPLE

In theory, an overnight stay at a Korean temple sounds like the perfect activity for anyone struggling to escape the pressures of modern life. You'll meditate, you'll learn about Buddhism, you'll go vegetarian. Concerns and cares will slip away as you drift into a blissful state of conscious awareness.

Unfortunately, that's not what it's like.

I signed up for one of these sleepovers through a program called Templestay. Created in 2002 by the Jogye Order of Korean Buddhism—the largest Buddhist order in Korea—the Templestay program aims to allow visitors to "sample ordained lifestyle and experience the mental training and cultural experience of Korea's ancient Buddhist tradition." In other words, it's a chance to test-drive life as a monk.

The meditation center I visited, about two hours from Seoul on Ganghwa Island, seemed like the sort of place that could inspire calm. The grounds are nestled between rice paddies and a leafy forest, and the center's brightly painted temple sits several stone steps up from a gentle brook and a small pond stocked with lotus flowers and koi.

When my friend and I arrived—several hours late, thanks to trouble reading the bus schedule—the Templestay coordinator introduced herself in fluent English and led us to the room where we'd be staying. It was empty except for sleeping pads, blankets, and small pillows stuffed with plastic beads (see nurdles, p. 101). After we'd dropped off our bags, she handed us our clothes for the weekend: two identical extra-large sets of baggy gray pants and vests, along with sun hats and blue plastic slippers. We looked like we'd stepped out of a propaganda poster for Maoist China.

I'd assumed that most temple life involved sitting still and cultivating enlightenment, but instead our first activity was community work time. Clad in our Mao suits, we followed the coordinator to the garden, where eight other Templestay guests squatted between raised rows of dirt, piles of potatoes scattered around them. They gave us hostile glances as we approached—thanks to our late arrival, they'd been forced to harvest potatoes for three hours in eighty-degree heat. I couldn't blame them for their animosity; if I'd been digging in the dirt while some assholes took the slow route to Ganghwa Island, I'd be pretty pissed off too. But such negativity seemed to go against the spirit of the retreat. I adjusted my sun hat and joined them in the field.

After we'd assumed our squatting positions, the coordinator explained that we were supposed to sort the potatoes into piles of small, medium, and large—and then left without demonstrating what the Buddhist definition of "small" was. After a half hour spent tossing any potato smaller than a golf ball into a nearby box, I looked up to find a monk standing above me, examining my work. I smiled. Expressionless, he picked up my box and emptied it onto the ground.

It was time for meditation.

Once we'd learned the correct way to arrange our shoes outside the temple door, the Templestay coordinator demonstrated how to prostrate according to the Korean Buddhist tradition: kneel down, touch your forehead to the floor, and rest your hands, palms upward, on the ground. Then do it all in reverse, like a movie playing backward. Repeat, ideally several hundred times.

To me, the main value of the prostration practice was as a quadriceps exercise, but any improvement in the shape of my thighs was mitigated by the pain it caused in my arthritic knees. I had plenty of time to reflect on this discomfort when we followed our prostrations with a meditation: sitting in silence for a half hour, a slight breeze blowing through the open doors at our back as if beckoning us to escape.

After a slow walking meditation through the temple grounds, a vegetarian dinner, calligraphy practice, and a discussion on meditation led by the temple's head monk (I spent most of the time killing mosquitoes and then feeling guilty about the karmic implications), we were sent back to our rooms to get rest before our 3:30 A.M. wake-up call. Lying on the floor, still dressed in my Mao suit, I fidgeted till 1:30.

Two hours later, the sound of the *mokt'ak*—a wooden percussion instrument played every morning to start the temple's day—jolted me awake. I pulled myself up from my floor mat and stumbled through the predawn darkness to the temple, where pink lotus lanterns illuminated a small group of people inside, creating the kind of picture you would send home to friends to make them feel jealous about the exotic experiences you had while on vacation.

There is a difference, however, between postcards and reality. For example, no one sends postcards at 3:30 in the morning. Nor do most people's vacation plans involve getting out of bed in the middle of the night to sit for a half hour in silence with their eyes closed. I watched through cracked eyelids as the Templestay coordinator repeatedly jerked herself awake just before tipping over, like a commuter on an early-morning subway train. I was close to succumbing to the same fate myself when I noticed something that kept me awake: a gigantic beetle crawling on a lotus lantern hanging above my head. This beetle was easily the size of a large fig; having it fall on my head would have been the equivalent of being smacked by a mouse. I began to focus my attention entirely on the beetle, sending prayers into the ether for its secure footing.

My prayers worked—the beetle remained aloft, and we were

eventually allowed to go back outside. After sneaking a cup of instant coffee with a Venezuelan couple, I pulled myself through another walking meditation and followed the other participants to the main room for a Buddhist meal ceremony. A highly choreographed process of place-setting, serving, and eating, it included a final inspection by a head monk to see if our bowls were clean. "You do not want to disappoint him," said the coordinator. "Doing so would reflect poorly."

She then walked us through what would take place during the meal ceremony, including a final cleansing: we were to take a piece of pickled radish and use it to swab our dishes. This caught the attention of a young Canadian woman.

"I'm sorry to interrupt," she said. "But how is wiping my bowl with a radish going to make it clean? What about germs?"

"We fill the bowls with very hot water," said the coordinator, sidestepping the question. "So when you use the radish, the bowl is already very clean."

"Is it, like, a hygienic radish?" asked the Canadian woman.

"Yes," said the coordinator. "It is a hygienic radish."

Things went downhill from there. Exhausted and cranky, one by one we began refusing to play monk. If one of the whole points of Buddhism was to cultivate acceptance, why, I asked, did we have to go through such an elaborate meal ceremony? The Venezuelan couple went a step further: they left.

Wishing that we had the same kind of courage, my friend and I instead counted down the hours until we returned to Seoul, and upon arrival treated ourselves to a bottle of wine. Several days later, the Templestay coordinator e-mailed the weekend's participants and invited us to a workshop to perform three thousand prostrations to "inspire yourself into practice." The idea sounded horrifying, but it reminded me how difficult it would be to live like a monk. Which, as the coordinator suggested, may have been the point.

14 PAMPLONA, FROM THE PERSPECTIVE OF A BULL

Pamplona •
Spain

Your day starts precisely at 8 A.M. when, standing in the pitch darkness of your temporary corral, you hear the sound of people singing. *"A San Fermín pedimos, por ser nuestro patrón, nos guíe en el encierro dándonos su bendición,"* they chant, asking a guy named Saint Fermín to give them his blessing as they participate in something called an "encierro."

"What's an 'encierro'?" you ask yourself, still sleepy from your long journey from your farm the day before. But before you get any answers, a gun goes off and someone presses a Taser to your skin, prodding you from complete darkness into total, blinding sunlight. Confused and frightened, you trip over your own hooves as you try to figure out what is going on. Your eyes adjust just in time to see a crowd of people, all dressed in white with silly red neckerchiefs, start to . . . hit you with rolled up newspapers? What the hell is this? And why are all the other bulls running so fast?

I'll tell you why: because those jerks with the newspapers are now chasing you down the street, whooping and hollering and poking you with their papers. "Really?" you think, hooves skittering on cobblestones as you force yourself around a corner. "Are you *really* trying to outrun a bull?"

It's enough to make you want to gore them, but there's no time— you've now reached a large ring and are surrounded by a different group of people, who force you into a new corral and give you some food. It tastes good, but man, it's making you sleepy. You haven't been this tired since that breakfast they gave you the day you left the farm. Maybe you'll just lie down for a little nap. . .

Suddenly it's 6:30 in the evening and you're being prodded back into that big circle, where thousands of people are staring down at you from the stands. Several men come up to you on horseback, but before you can figure out why the horses are wearing blindfolds, the men take sharp lancets and twist them into your neck and back muscles. What are they doing, trying to kill you? You try to raise your head to gore them, but the lancets are making it hard to move. You're

still really sleepy, the blood is flowing freely down your legs, a different man just came in and stuck a harpoon point in your back, and now some asshole is standing in front of you with a red cape.

This is officially the worst day ever.

Editor's note: In addition to the Running of the Bulls/subsequent nightly bullfights that occur in Pamplona during the eight days of the Fiesta de San Fermín, watch out for the People for the Ethical Treatment of Animals protest that occurs the day before the festival begins. Formerly known as the Running of the Nudes, it involves hundreds of naked people parading through the streets smeared with fake blood—and is a total buzzkill for anyone looking forward to the sight of drugged, wounded bulls being brutally slaughtered in front of a live audience.

15 THE GLOUCESTER CHEESE ROLLING COMPETITION

United Kingdom
Gloucester

Certain activities make me question how the human race survives. For example, the Cheese Rolling Competition, a yearly festival in which scores of people gather at Cooper's Hill near Gloucester, England, for the chance to chase a piece of cheese off a cliff. Bones are broken. Joints are dislocated. Contestants are carried off the field on stretchers. This might be understandable for a sufficiently large prize, but in this particular contest, runners are risking life and limb for the glory of winning a seven-pound round of Double Gloucester cheese.

Fans of the Cheese Rolling Competition will accuse me of oversimplifying things, so let me take a step back. The proud tradition of cheese rolling dates back some two hundred years (diehard fans insist it comes from the Romans) and follows a strict order of proceedings. First, competitors line up on the top of Cooper's Hill, a rugged, uneven pitch so steep that from the top of the slope, it appears concave. A master of ceremonies, wearing a white coat and a silly hat, escorts a guest "roller"—the person responsible for releasing the cheese—to the edge of the hill. On the count of three, the roller releases the cheese; on the fourth count, the runners throw themselves down the hill after it. Originally the point was to try to catch the cheese, but given that it can travel more than seventy miles per hour and has a one-second head start, the winner is usually just whoever crosses the finish line first.

It's a painful race to watch. Most people lose their footing almost immediately and begin violently tumbling down the hill, bouncing onto shoulders, ankles, and heads, occasionally landing back on their feet before being thrown forward again. Lucky runners make it to the bottom intact, where volunteer rugby players known as catchers try to intercept them before they crash into the safety barrier of hay bales. Unlucky contestants are taken away by ambulance.

The 2009 competition alone saw fifty-nine injuries, of which only thirty-five were competitors. The rest were catchers and spectators, some trampled, some wounded when hit by the wayward cheese. One particularly unfortunate man held up the entire contest when he fell out of a tree.

But regardless of its inherent dangers, history dictates that the competition must continue. When World War II rationing forbade using a real round of cheese, contest organizers fashioned a cheese-shaped piece of wood with a token piece of Gloucester stowed inside. And even when the contest itself has been canceled, as it was during the foot-and-mouth scare of 2001 and again in 2003 when the contest's volunteer Search and Rescue Assistance in Disasters teams were called off to help victims of an Algerian earthquake, organizers rolled a single piece of cheese off the hill anyway—a symbolic act to ensure that the tradition would remain unbroken. If only the same were true for contestants' bones.

✕✕ MICHAEL AND ISAAC POLLAN ✕✕

The Worst Meal in Barcelona

It'd be hard to pinpoint the best meal in Barcelona, a city known for its excellent Catalonian food. But on a recent trip there, our family had no trouble identifying the worst: a frozen, microwaveable paella—basically, a Spanish TV dinner—available in low-end eateries near tourist destinations. A true paella is a delicious thing, a saffron-infused concoction of meats, vegetables, or seafood cooked with rice in a two-handled pan over an open flame until the ingredients are tender and the bottom has formed a savory crust. Unfortunately, however, the dish does not stand up well in the microwave.

We had ours one hot afternoon after leaving the Park Güell, Gaudí's weirdly wonderful garden on a hill overlooking the city. We left the park around 4 p.m., famished, and could find no other place willing to serve lunch; the kitchens were closed. But not the microwaves at the place near the trinket shop. There they offered several versions of traditional foods—various tapas and raciónes and, of course, my fateful paella. I placed my order, and in the kitchen, out of sight, someone slipped it into the microwave. Several minutes later, my Spanish meal was served.

What possessed me to order it? A desire to have something indigenous, I suppose. But there was nothing indigenous about the substance on the steaming plate before me: it was a solid clump of mushy rice punctuated with dubious chunks of sausage and a few world-weary prawns.

I should have gone with the hot dog.

MICHAEL POLLAN is the author of *The Omnivore's Dilemma: A Natural History of Four Meals* and *In Defense of Food: An Eater's Manifesto.*

Before heading to Barcelona, my parents and I had received lists from many esteemed culinary minds as to where to spend each bite in the tapas capital of the world. But these lists did us no good when, walking back to the Metro from Park Güell, the three of us were simultaneously struck by pangs of late-afternoon hunger. I knew what this meant: far from any foodie destination, we would have to venture into a restaurant unexplored by our gourmand guides. There would be no Alice Waters in the back of our heads recommending the "ever-so-simple" tomato breads and the Iberico ham, or Dan Barber advising us to try the fried artichokes with the lemon aioli, or even my grandmother suggesting the Pimientos de Padrón. We were truly on our own.

The restaurant we found was so bland that it didn't even have a name. And yet this was our only choice; it was siesta, and the other shops we passed were closed. Except, of course, for this anonymous hole in the wall, which we staggered into upon spying paella on the crookedly taped menu in the front window.

As we entered we were quickly greeted and ushered to a table that was squeezed so tightly into a corner that it reminded me of a Tetris piece. I sat down and immediately noticed three ominous things: the tableware and chairs (all plastic), the fact that there was not a single Spaniard in the entire establishment, and the bathroom. Oh, the bathroom. It wasn't politely located down the hall or in the back; no, it sat in the corner across from our table, in the dining room itself. Consisting of three small walls erected to form a box the size of a small airport bathroom stall, it leaked both smells and sounds.

But despite all of this, the actual items on the menu did not seem too nauseating. My parents, emboldened by their hunger, ordered the surf and turf paellas. I stuck to the strictly turf. After placing our order with a middle-aged and chipper man, we waited for five, ten, twenty minutes, our stomachs growling louder and louder until I was sure the entire restaurant could hear the symphony of our gastric tracts. Then, finally, the food arrived, delivered in three matching oval plastic plates with slightly elevated walls.

I stared, crestfallen at the sight of my dish. It was a large lump of brown-black gooeyness, with indecipherable chunks jutting out from the sludge. Upon the first bite, which required me to cram my plastic fork as hard as possible into the slightly crusty edges of the dish, I came to the conclusion that my paella had been frozen for a very, very long time. Perhaps the delay in service was due to the time it took our server to find an ice pick to extricate the dish from the bottom of his freezer.

But while disgusting, no one could accuse my paella of being simple. After a top note of freezer burn came the lovely astringent taste of gamy meat and mushy carrot. The rice was even more complex: clumped and congealed, certain bites were reminiscent of leather-hard slabs of clay. Others were mushy beyond recognition, saturated with a drool-like substance released from the meat that created an effect of heavily burnt oatmeal.

I've never seen my father so happy to pay the bill.

—ISAAC POLLAN

✕✕✕✕

WALL DRUG

South Dakota

United States

If you've taken a cross-country road trip, chances are you've seen the signs. At its peak in the 1960s, Wall Drug—a roadside attraction in South Dakota that has become synonymous with American kitsch—was advertised on over three thousand billboards around the country. HAVE YOU DUG WALL DRUG? FREE COFFEE AND DONUT FOR VETERANS: WALL DRUG. T-REX: WALL DRUG.

The signs were so relentless that Wall Drug became a tautology of a tourist trap: a place worth visiting only because of the billboards claiming it was worth visiting. Adding to the circularity, the advertisements themselves are now considered campy artifacts in their own right, and have sprung up in places as far away from South Dakota as Moscow, the Taj Mahal, Afghanistan, and even the South Pole.

These days the actual Wall Drug advertises itself as a "76,000 square foot wonderland of free attractions" including both a life-size tyrannosaurus rex head and the world's second-largest fiberglass jackalope. But it wasn't always this glamorous: when the original Wall Drug opened in 1931, Wall was a tiny prairie town with fewer than four hundred residents. Wall Drug's founders, Ted Hustead and his wife, Dorothy, liked the town because it had a drugstore for sale and a Catholic church. Their families, however, were not as easily convinced, and insisted on having a prayer circle to see if it was really a good idea. Luckily for lovers of American roadside attractions, God approved.

It takes a while, though, to go from a small family-run pharmacy to an internationally known destination, and for a while, business was slow—really slow. So slow that even five years after they'd opened—Dorothy and Ted's self-imposed deadline to turn things around—it still was virtually nonexistent. And then one hot summer day Dorothy, watching passing carloads of sweaty travelers, stumbled upon a gimmick that, in retrospect, was genius: Wall Drug should give away free ice water.

Dorothy even came up with a slogan: "Get a soda . . . Get a root

he Jackalope

beer . . . Turn next corner . . . Just as near . . . To Highway 16 & 14 . . . Free Ice Water . . . Wall Drug." Skeptical but supportive, Ted got a kid to help him paint the slogan on a bunch of wooden signs, then spent a weekend nailing them up on the side of the road, spaced out so that travelers could read them sequentially as they drove. According to legend, by the time he got back to the store, people were already lining up for ice water.

That Wall Drug still exists is a testament to how few manmade tourist attractions there are in South Dakota (cf., Mount Rushmore, p. 92). But it's also a testament to clever advertising and ice cubes. Seventy-something years since Ted and Dorothy opened their shop, Wall Drug now is a sprawling cowboy-themed mall with restaurants, gift shops, a chapel, an art museum, and attractions that include a piano-playing gorilla and an eighty-foot-tall apatosaurus. You can buy boot spurs or a "freedom pistol," watch some singing cowboy dolls, or take a photo of your kids on the jackalope. Wall Drug still offers free ice water and 5-cent cups of coffee, but that's about all that is recognizable from the original tiny store. It's grown so large that it is no longer simply an attraction—Wall Drug has swallowed the town.

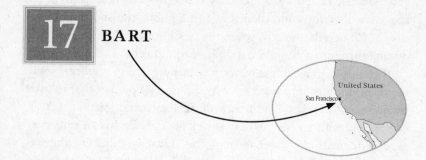

17 BART

United States

San Francisco

L et's start with the carpet. Why would Bay Area Rapid Transit, one of the country's busiest commuter rail systems, decide it was a good idea to upholster the floor?

The result is Eau de BART, the stomach-turning scent that hits you in the face every time you board a train to San Francisco. It's a blend of spilled coffee, greasy hair, body odor left by vagrants who take naps on its blue cloth seats, and the aroma that arises from substances trapped on thousands of commuters' shoes. Thankfully, there's a movement afoot to rip up the rug from some of the cars, but this still leaves the question of the fabric seats unresolved. Perhaps my allegiance to the New York subway system makes me biased, but I believe that all public transportation systems should be built with materials that can be hosed down with bleach.

BART was honored as one of the Top Ten Public Works Projects of the Century by the American Public Works Association. But despite this accolade, its problems don't end with its odor—or with the questionable decision to refer to a major public transportation system with an acronym that rhymes with "fart." BART is the main transit link between the East Bay and San Francisco, and yet its trains don't run between 12 and 4 A.M. Berkeley residents looking for a night on the town therefore find themselves in a public transportation version of Cinderella—except when the clock strikes midnight, BART doesn't turn into a pumpkin; it disappears entirely.

If you do manage to get on a train, be prepared to ponder several engineering questions such as: why did no one predict that thanks to some unfortunate confluence of acoustics and friction, BART cars would emit an ear-piercing shriek for their entire 3.6-mile passage underneath the water through the Transbay Tube? Or, alternatively, what would happen in an earthquake? The BART Earthquake Safety Program has identified areas that are particularly vulnerable if the ground starts to shake: the Transbay Tube, the stations, and the aerial guideways that prop up the tracks when the train emerges above ground. In other words, pretty much all of it. One can only hope that if and when the big one comes, it does so between the hours of midnight and 4 A.M.

18   A STOP ON CARRY NATION'S HATCHETATION TOUR

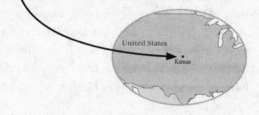

United States

Kansas

Born in 1846, Carry Nation didn't come from the stablest of backgrounds. Her maternal grandmother, aunt, uncle, and cousin all had dementia, and her mother suffered from delusions that she was Queen Victoria. Not to be outdone, Nation directed her own mental energy toward religion; she claimed to have frequent chats with Jesus.

Apparently, Jesus had a lot to say about alcohol. After her first husband drank himself to death, Nation remarried and joined the Women's Christian Temperance Union, which closed all liquor-selling establishments in Medicine Lodge, Kansas, except for one stubborn drugstore. The other women considered this a success, but it wasn't enough for Nation, who grabbed a sledgehammer, stormed into the shop, and smashed a keg of whiskey. The druggist, terrified, left soon thereafter, and Nation had found herself a cause.

After following a voice in her head that told her to destroy saloons in nearby Kiowa, Nation returned to Medicine Lodge and bought a hatchet. She then began what she called a "hatchetation" tour across the eastern half of the United States, bursting into saloons and destroying bottles with an enthusiastic chant of "Smash! Smash! For Jesus' sake, smash!" Nation soon developed such a formidable reputation that when she arrived in New York City, bartenders locked their doors. Who could blame them? The woman was nearly six feet tall, a muscular 175 pounds, armed, and crazy.

Luckily, Nation kept her rampages focused on inanimate objects like bottles, kegs, and cash registers; her reign of terror ended when she ran out of money and was reduced to supporting herself by selling souvenir hatchets and reenacting saloon smashes at local carnivals. But her legacy lived on—and across the United States, bartenders posted signs in her honor. ALL NATIONS SERVED, they said. EXCEPT CARRY.

Carry Nation with bible, hatchet

THE THIRD INFILTRATION
TUNNEL AT THE DMZ

N. Korea

S. Korea

Advertised by tourist brochures as the "most fortified border on Earth that only Korea can offer," the demilitarized zone is anthropologically fascinating, not to mention one of the world's only active battle lines to have its own gift shop. (Sample souvenirs: DMZ key chains, child-size camouflage suits, duty-free alcohol.) There is a welcome center; there is a movie theater. Concerned about providing fodder for North Korean propaganda photos, the DMZ even has its own dress code; visitors are forbidden from wearing flip-flops, tank tops, or shorts that "expose the buttocks." It is not entirely clear what the people who wrote the dress code have against leather riding chaps, but they're not kidding: wear the wrong thing, and you're not going on the tour.

Providing that your pants meet protocol, you'll sign a release acknowledging that you could get shot, watch a slideshow presentation and briefing, and eventually be led to the Joint Security Area, which is the only area in the DMZ where North and South Korean troops stand face-to-face.

The border in this section is less Berlin Wall than it is sidewalk curb: a half foot tall and straddled by a group of squat, powder-blue UN buildings. These were originally designed as neutral spots for negotiations. But since visitors are allowed to go inside, most of the negotiations going on these days are among members of large tour groups figuring out where in the building they need to stand to get a picture of themselves in what is technically North Korea. Like most of the DMZ tour, this comes highly recommended. But do not bother with the Third Infiltration Tunnel.

That's not because it is uninteresting. The Third Infiltration Tunnel—or the Third Tunnel of Aggression, as it's more poetically known—is the third discovered underground passageway (of an estimated dozen or so) that North Korea's Kim Jong Il ordered to be blasted from North to South Korea in preparation for a potential invasion. When South Korea found this particular tunnel in 1978, North Korea claimed that it was merely a coal mine—even going so far as to have part of the granite walls painted black. Unconvinced, the South blocked the tunnel with three barricades and then, as a capitalist "screw you," opened it as a tourist site.

The resulting experience is not for claustrophobics, people prone to panic attacks, or anyone with an aversion to being buried alive. First, you're led to a train platform and told to put all your belongings into a small cubby. Next, you're given a hard hat and herded onto a small trolley. That's probably the part where you should start asking questions, like: why are you on a train? Or, more important, where are you going? But most tourists, lulled into complacence by the trolley's similarity to those in Disneyland's "It's a Small World," don't think to be inquisitive.

Instead, the claustrophobic visitor will experience an unexpected rush of terror as the train begins a 240-foot descent underground through a narrow tunnel blasted out of solid rock. As your little train chugs lower and lower, you wonder how the giggling tourists around you can seem so oblivious to the lack of emergency exits and escape hatches built into the suffocating walls pushing in on you from all sides. Several horrible minutes later, the trolley finally reaches the bottom and you're given several minutes to walk to the tunnel's main attraction—the barricade between North and South Korea. (Spoiler alert: it looks like a wall.) The good part about the tunnel is that, at 6½ by 6½ feet, it's slightly less oppressive than the train ride, but the extra headroom isn't worth the panic attack it took to get there.

Your opinion toward bus travel in Samoa is likely to depend on one important variable: whether or not you mind being close with strangers. And when I say close, I'm not talking about having your face smushed into people's armpits during rush hour. I'm talking about sitting on their laps.

In Samoa, buses are small, seating is limited, and nobody's supposed to stand. So drivers are left with two options: leave people in the road, or assume the passengers will find a place for them to sit. Etiquette dictates the latter, and so whenever a bus picks up someone—which could be anywhere, since Samoa has few predetermined bus stops—the passengers engage in a round of quiet shuffling to make space on someone's lap for the new arrival. Whose lap you sit on depends on your status in the social hierarchy—elderly people get the front, then come women with children, then women with no children, and finally a throng of men at the back.

If you have a loose definition of personal boundaries, this lap sitting can actually be a fun cultural experience, not to mention provide a welcome layer of padding on rough roads. But be careful: according to the World Health Organization, in Samoan urban areas, over 75 percent of adults are obese. Ending up on the wrong side of a lap could mean a very painful ride.

Also worth noting: After years of driving on the right, Samoans recently were forced to start driving on the left, a transition that not only increases the risk of head-on collisions, but means that many bus doors now open directly into oncoming traffic.

The Tupperware Museum

America has an enduring passion for highly specific and unnecessary food storage receptacles. It was created, almost single handedly, by Earl Tupper, the man whose Orlando empire has given us, over the years, the Garlic Keeper and the specially designed pickle storage container, never minding that the Vlasic jar has a screwable lid. I once wrote a magazine article about Tupperware, partly because I was fascinated by Mr. Tupper and his wares, but also because I had long harbored a desire, unfathomable even to me, to visit the Tupperware Museum of Historical Food Containers. Could anything be duller? (Possibly. There's a Needle Museum somewhere in England.)

As the afternoon at Tupperware HQ wound down and my host from the public relations office began moving us toward the door, I asked to be directed to the museum. She replied that it had closed some years back and that the contents were—are you ready?—*in storage*.

Years later, I found a photograph of the museum. Its dullness surpassed even my imagination: brown carpeting and case after case of drab, unimaginatively displayed crockery, amphoras, vats. It appeared that the whole point of the museum had been to make pre-Tupperware food storage seem sad and boring, to foster a yearning for festively colored Wonderlier bowls and stackable sandwich-fixings holders. Nonetheless, my disappointment lingers, as though for all these years it had been stored in a virtually airtight, just-right Disappointment Keeper.

MARY ROACH is the author of *Spook: Science Tackles the Afterlife.*

XXXX

21 AN OUTDOOR WEDDING DURING THE 2021 EMERGENCE OF THE GREAT EASTERN CICADA BROOD

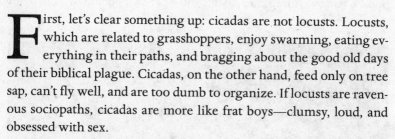

First, let's clear something up: cicadas are not locusts. Locusts, which are related to grasshoppers, enjoy swarming, eating everything in their paths, and bragging about the good old days of their biblical plague. Cicadas, on the other hand, feed only on tree sap, can't fly well, and are too dumb to organize. If locusts are ravenous sociopaths, cicadas are more like frat boys—clumsy, loud, and obsessed with sex.

There are cicadas around every year, but the number of annual cicadas is nothing compared to their periodical counterparts, which are the longest-living insects in North America and only exist in the eastern United States. These periodical cicadas spend most of their lives underground, but every thirteen or seventeen years, depending on the species, entire broods of cicadas push their way out of the dirt and climb into trees to mate. Scientists don't know how cicadas synchronize their appearance—it might be related to soil temperature—but the result is striking: millions of cicadas can come out of the ground in a single night.

Once above ground, cicadas devote themselves to one thing:

finding another cicada. Newly emerged cicadas, still nymphs, climb up on whatever woody structures they can find and quickly molt into adults, leaving behind amber-colored, creepy-looking sheaths that are great for practical jokes. Then the males start singing, joining together in chirping choruses that can reach up to 100 dB. Females respond by coyly flicking their wings, and about ten days of nonstop noise later, they mate. Females cut slits in twigs, lay eggs, and then die, their carcasses dropping from trees to form a thick, crunchy carpet. Six or seven weeks later, tiny white ant-like nymphs hatch, fall to the ground, burrow into the dirt, and the cycle begins again.

So let's get to the wedding: the Great Eastern Brood, also known as Brood X, is the farthest-reaching cicada brood in the northeastern United States—and it's set for a reemergence in 2021. Sometime early that summer—probably in the heat of wedding season—millions of cicadas will tunnel their way toward open air and, if you plan things poorly, your wedding site. Imagine it: your vows being drowned out

by the singing of thousands of horny cicadas, insects falling onto your guests' heads, the crunch underfoot of countless abandoned shells.

The upside is that cicadas are harmless—they don't bite or sting, and they're not even attracted to human food. But at 1½ inches long with large wings and bright red eyes, they're definitely noticeable, especially given their tendency to fly into things. If your wedding site has seen cicadas in the past, consider renting a tent.

22 (TR)ACTION PARK

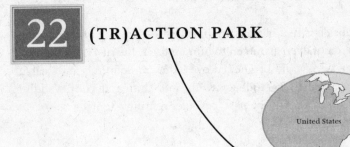

United States
New Jersey

Action Park—also known as Traction Park, Class Action Park, and Death Park—was an amusement park in Vernon Township, New Jersey. Responsible for at least six deaths and countless accidents, it inspired so many personal injury lawsuits that in 1996, it was forced to shut down.

The park was built as an off-season moneymaker for the Vernon Valley/Great Gorge ski area, and featured rides so obviously dangerous that they call into question the sanity of the person who designed them. Take, for example, the Alpine Slide. Built into the ski slope, it sent visitors zooming down the hillside on a concrete and fiberglass track in sleds equipped with poorly maintained brakes. There were two speeds available: very slow or extremely fast. Extremely fast meant risking having your sled jump the rails (a frequent occurrence), suffering abrasions and burns when you hit the track, and being hurled into a bale of hay at the bottom of the hill. Very slow, on the other hand, put you in danger of being rear-ended by the extremely fast person behind you. In 1984 and 1985, state records show that the ride resulted in at least fourteen fractures and twenty-six head injuries. It was also responsible for the park's first death.

But the accidents didn't stop there. Employees—mostly under twenty years old and often inebriated—souped up the Super Go Karts so that guests could play bumper cars at fifty miles per hour. The Super Speedboats, which visitors often rammed into one another, shared a pond with a healthy population of water snakes. The Tidal Wave Pool—nicknamed the "Grave Pool"—required twelve full-time lifeguards, who reported rescuing as many as thirty people per day on busy summer weekends. The Tarzan Swing dropped people into a pool of water so cold that in 1984, it's said to have triggered a man's fatal heart attack. The Aqua Scoot gave people head lacerations. The Diving Cliffs were positioned above a pool whose swimmers didn't know they existed. The Kayak Experience's submerged electric fans killed the park's second victim: a twenty-seven-year-old man who was electrocuted when his boat tipped over and he stepped out to right it.

And then there was the Cannonball Loop slide—an enclosed waterslide that ended with a roller coaster-esque loop-de-loop. Based on the faulty premise that a wet bathing suit would provide the slickness and momentum necessary to carry a person up and around a 360-degree loop, the ride was closed after only a month.

Gone are the days of Action Park's treacherous rides, untrained employees, and copious beer stands. It's now the Mountain Creek Waterpark and is, by all accounts, much, much safer. But the morbidly nostalgic can still catch a glimpse of past dangers—underneath the route of the modern-day gondola lies the abandoned track of the Alpine Slide.

23 A GIANT ROOM FILLED WITH HUMAN CRAP

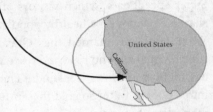

Imagine a room filled with human shit—huge, steaming piles of it, arranged in rows in a dimly lit, windowless space the size of a parking garage. Actively rotting, the piles give off a fog so thick that, on particularly humid days, the machinery operators can't actually see the ground.

Sound appealing? The Inland Empire Regional Composting Authority is the country's largest indoor composting facility for biosolids—a fancy word for sewage sludge. Housed in a former Ikea warehouse, the facility gets its raw material from an area in Southern California called the Inland Empire, blends the sludge with wood chips, lets it rot, and sells it as SoilPro, a fertilizer for home gardens.

By the end of its sixty-day journey through the warehouse, microbes have broken the sludge down so thoroughly that it's recognizable only by a faded manure-like smell and dark brown color. But there is nothing subtle about the process it took to get there. In the main composting room, which is a vast cavern bathed in dim yellow light, mounds of steaming sludge stretch toward the ceiling in piles taller than the trucks that brought them in. A system of powerful fans changes the room's air twelve times an hour, but the smell is still so strong that stepping out of your car's protective bubble for even a moment will burn your eyes, turn your stomach, and saturate your clothing with the scent of ammonia and excrement.

A warehouse full of rotting feces. You had me at "Hello."

Steaming piles of poop

24 KINGMAN REEF

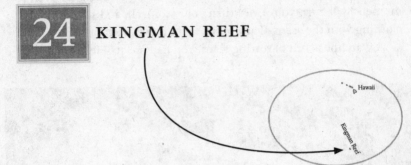

Hawaii

Kingman Reef

There are places you should stay away from because they're not worth the trouble, and there are places to stay away from because if humans visit, things get screwed up. Kingman Reef qualifies on both counts.

Smack in the middle of the Pacific Ocean, Kingman Reef is about a thousand miles from Honolulu. Technically it's the northernmost of the Line Islands, but that's a dubious nomenclature since it's not actually an island. Above water, Kingman Reef is an uninhabited spit of smashed coral and shells, decorated by occasional pieces of human-made flotsam: plastic bottles, broken bits of Styrofoam, and a shocking number of widowed flip-flops. Its total land area is about 0.01 square miles.

When I visited the reef on a two-week marine biology expedition from the Line Islands to Hawaii, the first thing I noticed as our boat approached was a shipwreck washed up on the spit's opposite shore. At first this seemed cool—a shipwreck! How fun! Then I remembered that I was on a boat. I also noticed the mood of our captain, who was becoming increasingly nervous as we neared the spit. Unable to drop anchor—he didn't want to damage any coral—he was guiding us back and forth along a line, motoring the ship a safe distance away from land, killing the engine, letting us drift back toward shore, and then starting the motor again. He did this for sixteen hours.

Meanwhile, the marine biologists in charge of the expedition decided that our proximity to the reef was the perfect occasion for a new evening activity: shark baiting. Who cared that it was beginning to storm? Using the remnants of a tuna they had caught several days before, the crew spent the night dangling chunks of flesh off the side of the boat, tempting sharks—of which there were many— to approach our boat and jump through the horizontal rain as they tried to snap the fish off the line.

By the following morning, the captain's nerves were shot. He suggested leaving, but the marine biologists had other things in mind. Namely, snorkeling. To avoid tempting the sharks, we went out in large inflatable rafts, leaned out over the edge, and stuck our heads in the water.

Which brings me to the second reason not to visit: Kingman Reef is beautiful. Stick your head underwater and you'll be treated to the sight of bright corals, giant clams, and countless fish; I even caught sight of a camouflaged octopus hiding in the seaweed. According to marine biologists, Kingman Reef is one of perhaps fifty reefs worldwide that have been preserved in such a pristine condition, free from human interference and pollution. The result is a spectacular sight, but also means that, for the reef's own sake, we shouldn't go see it.

NAKED SUSHI

Do your favorite things in the world include fish, seaweed, and sex? Do you love sushi but wish it could be a little rawer?

Then find a restaurant that offers *nyotaimori*. Literally translated as "female body presentation," *nyotaimori* is colloquially known as "naked sushi": raw fish served on a nude woman.

After stripping down and shaving off all extraneous body hair, young, nubile models wash themselves in unscented soap, lie down on a table, and allow chefs to cover them in sushi, seaweed, and a few strategically placed flowers. Wheeled into a banquet room, they then spend several hours staring blankly at the ceiling as diners ogle their bodies and poke them with chopsticks. In places with particularly strict hygiene laws—not to mention interesting interpretations of what qualifies as sexy—the models are covered in saran wrap.

To an outsider, *nyotaimori* might just seem like an example of sitophila—the desire to eat foods off another person's body. But fans insist it's actually a matter of taste; by sitting for a half hour on a woman's bare stomach, they explain, your tuna roll is heated to body temperature. According to their logic, this allows its flavors to expand and prevents the unpleasant shock that comes when the fish is too cold. One could argue that since belly buttons are not the most efficient chafers—that's why God invented heat lamps—the true appeal is less about temperature than titillation. Fair enough, say its fans. Fewer people means a better view.

Nyotaimori, which started in Japan, has been banned in China for "insult[ing] people's moral quality." So instead the phenomenon spread east. *Nyotaimori* bars can be found in cities including Los Angeles, Chicago, New York, and, yes, Minneapolis. Some American bars also offer *nantaimori*: sushi served on a naked man.

But despite its questionable morals and hygiene, *nyotaimori* is not the grossest Japanese food custom out there. That honor goes to *wakame sake*. Translated as seaweed sake, it's a delicacy where a naked, supine model clamps her thighs together to form a triangular cup. Sake is poured down her body and into the indentation. As it fills, the woman's pubic hair begins to gently undulate in the warm sake, similar—say the poets—to seaweed swaying in the ocean. Then a drunk businessman leans down and slurps it out of her crotch.

Delicious.

26 ORGAN PIPE CACTUS NATIONAL MONUMENT

Situated on the U.S.-Mexico border in Arizona, Organ Pipe Cactus National Monument is a 330,689-acre piece of the Sonoran Desert best known not just for its wildlife or iconic organ-pipe cacti but for its status as a border crossing for drug traffickers. The U.S. Park Rangers Lodge of the Fraternal Order of Police named Organ Pipe the most dangerous national park in the United States, and *National Geographic* describes it as a place where park rangers "wear camouflage, carry assault rifles, and chase drug smugglers through the blazing desert." "They're at the front lines of a violent border war," says the magazine, "and they're losing." In 2002, a twenty-eight-year-old ranger was shot and killed while attempting to help border control agents catch two men suspected in a drug-related quadruple murder, and in 2002, rangers seized 14,000 pounds of pot from the park—a third of the total seized in all national parks and monuments combined.

This doesn't deter visitors—with up to one thousand guests per night, Organ Pipe leads the national parks in the number of back-country stays. Granted, most of those visitors have entered the

United States illegally through the park's thirty-one-mile border with Mexico (park rangers advise what to do if you come across people in distress asking for food and water). But if they're willing to deal with the desert's 116-degree summer heat, venomous snakes, spiders, scorpions, centipedes, and, of course, drug traffickers, perhaps it's only fair to let them stay the night.

TIMES SQUARE ON NEW YEAR'S EVE

There are only two circumstances where a dropping ball can qualify as a noteworthy event: male adolescence and New Year's Eve in Times Square. Having had no personal experience with the first, I will instead skip to the second and say that if you value your sanity, your extremities, and your bladder, you should find a different place to celebrate the new year.

The tradition goes back to 1904, when Adolph S. Ochs, owner of the *New York Times*, threw a party on New Year's Eve to celebrate the opening of the newspaper's headquarters at what is now One Times Square. With an all-day street festival and a thrilling fireworks display, Ochs's party was so successful that it quickly became New York's premier New Year's Eve party.

The New Year's ball didn't come into play till 1907, however, when Ochs commissioned a 700-pound iron-and-wood ball with one hundred 25-watt lightbulbs to be lowered from the tower's flagpole to celebrate 1908. Since then it's been replaced several times—1920 introduced a 400-pound ball made of wrought iron; 1955 saw the debut of a 150-pound aluminum sphere. In 1980, red lightbulbs and a stem turned the ball into an apple for the "I Love New York" marketing campaign, and the millennium celebration was graced by a ball made from Waterford Crystal. In 2009, the co-organizers of the celebration unveiled the latest ball: twelve feet in diameter, it's covered in crystals and more than thirty-two thousand LEDs. At around six tons, it puts previous balls to shame.

But even a six-ton ball is not enough to justify spending your New Year's Eve in the Square. Back in the good old days, drunken revelers packed themselves behind wooden barriers, partied their hearts out, and then hopped back on the Long Island Railroad. Nowadays the event is heavily guarded by the NYPD, with each partygoer treated as a possible member of Al Qaeda. Backpacks and large bags are forbidden, and every would-be reveler has to pass through a metal detector before being allowed into the Square.

Once inside (and get there early, since people start arriving by midday), you're stuck: in order to control the crowd and prevent people from pressing to the front, the police herd visitors into metal pens, which they're not allowed to leave until the clock strikes twelve. If you do desert your fellow ~~livestock~~ partygoers, don't expect to get back to your original spot—by midnight, the streets are packed to Penn Station, eight blocks away.

And trust me when I say you'll have plenty of reasons to leave. First, it's freezing. January in New York is cold, and midnight in January in New York is even colder. The event organizers recommend dressing in heavy layers, but I'd go a step further and suggest wearing everything you own.

It'd be nice if you could warm up with a cup of soup, but don't get your hopes up: food vendors aren't allowed in the Square on New Year's Eve. So unless you packed your pockets with Clif Bars or feel like paying a cover charge at a restaurant (and thus losing your place in the pen), you're going to be ringing in the new year on an empty stomach.

You're also going to be celebrating it sober—at the world's most famous New Year's party, no alcohol is allowed. Some people choose to booze it up ahead of time—like at 10 A.M.—but be careful: there are no bathrooms. That's right. Nearly a million people crowd into Times Square every New Year's Eve, some of whom arrive twelve hours before the ball drops, and yet the city provides no additional facilities. In the words of a former NYPD cop, if you want to survive New Year's in Times Square, "you'd better have the bladder of a camel."

If you are still insistent on spending New Year's Eve in Times Square (perhaps you are also the sort of person who enjoys spending long periods of time in MRI tubes), then do yourself a favor and get a hotel room with a view of the festivities. It'll be expensive, and you'll have to book far in advance, but when you're standing in your toasty room, champagne glass in hand, looking down at the crowds with a private toilet just steps away, there'll be no question it was worth it.

28 THE DOUBLE BLACK DIAMOND RUN AT POWDERHOUSE HILL

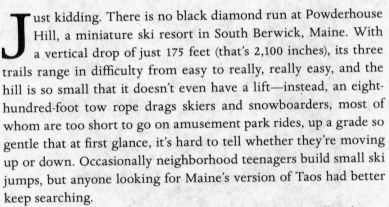

Just kidding. There is no black diamond run at Powderhouse Hill, a miniature ski resort in South Berwick, Maine. With a vertical drop of just 175 feet (that's 2,100 inches), its three trails range in difficulty from easy to really, really easy, and the hill is so small that it doesn't even have a lift—instead, an eight-hundred-foot tow rope drags skiers and snowboarders, most of whom are too short to go on amusement park rides, up a grade so gentle that at first glance, it's hard to tell whether they're moving up or down. Occasionally neighborhood teenagers build small ski jumps, but anyone looking for Maine's version of Taos had better keep searching.

If you're not a thrill-seeker, however, Powderhouse Hill is charming. Run entirely by volunteers, lift tickets go for $5, and $25 earns you a lifetime membership. The small chalet at the bottom of the hill is heated by a wood stove and sells small snacks to offset the cost of running the ski area. The best part: the original engine for the tow rope came courtesy of a jerry-rigged 1938 Ford truck that the founders of the ski slope parked on the top of the hill and modified so that its rear wheel could pull the rope. These days its engine has been replaced by a newer, thirty-seven-horsepower version, but the truck still sits at the top of the hill, chugging away.

29 THE DOUBLE BLACK DIAMOND RUN AT CORBET'S COULOIR

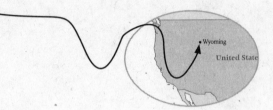

Powderhouse Hill might not be great for thrill-seekers, but conversely, Corbet's Couloir in Jackson Hole, Wyoming, is a must-miss spot for anyone who would prefer not to meet their doom on skis.

Ranked fourth on *Skiing Magazine*'s 2006 list of "Top 50 Things ALL Skiers Must Do Before They Die," the couloir sits at the top of Jackson Hole's Rendezvous Mountain, which has the greatest continuous rise of any ski slope in the United States. If you scoot yourself up to the edge of the couloir, you'll see a narrow chute lined with jagged rocks, but be careful. The first person to ski Corbet's was a ski patroller who accidentally fell into it after the cornice he was standing on collapsed.

Skiers who push themselves off the edge deliberately have a ten- to thirty-foot leap of faith (i.e., free fall) onto a fifty-five-degree slope, at which point they have to immediately hit a very hard right turn, lest they "smash into a face of Precambrian rock," as one Corbet survivor described it. The chute eventually flattens to a mere forty-five-degree angle, but few people even make it to that point; watch videos of Corbet attempts and you'll acquire a newfound appreciation for the many different ways in which one can wipe out on skis.

These videos also give a vivid example of how easily humans—especially those who are young and male—can be convinced to do stupid things. My favorite begins with a group of college-aged guys standing at the top of the cliff asking one another if he is going to ski it. "Fuck that," says one. "I kind of want to vomit," says another. Then someone hurls himself off the edge. His buddies, now convinced that not jumping off the cliff will mean they have no testicles, follow. The next scene is in a hospital.

But despite the toll Corbet's must take on Jackson Hole's ski patrol, the mountain itself is making a profit off of those foolish enough to attempt the run. A special Steep and Deep Ski Camp offers elite skiers a chance to spend four days on a guide-assisted program tackling some of Jackson Hole's most challenging terrain, culminating in a chance to try Corbet's. Proof of how reckless one must be to ski it: despite having paid nearly a thousand dollars to participate in the program, most Steep and Deep participants decide not to try.

If we expand our stupid-places-to-ski adventure outside the United States, the editors at Skiing Magazine *have told me there is one clear winner: Bec des Rosses in Vernier, Switzerland. It's home of a yearly Xtreme Verbier Freeride event that's considered the most prestigious in the world. Imagine skiing down one of the mountains on an Evian bottle: a 1,650-foot north face, lots of exposed rock, and a slope that gets up to fifty-five degrees (that is, when you're not in free fall). As professional skier Shroder Baker put it, "It's a huge cheese-grating monster, with sharp jagged rocks all the way down."*

THE *BEAST*

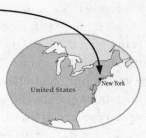

United States   New York

S ome visitors to New York enjoy viewing the city skyline from the tranquil deck of the Circle Line Sightseeing cruise ship; others prefer to spend their time in the Big Apple puking over the edge of speedboats. Or at least that's the only explanation I've come up with for the continued popularity of the *Beast*, a motorboat painted to resemble an open-mouthed shark that gives daily "water coaster" rides through New York Harbor. "With over 90 speakers, Captain 'Mad Dog' pumps up the crowd with popular music and amusing New York 'shtick 'throughout the ride," the *Beast*'s promoters boast. Translation? You will be forced to sing along to "Eye of the Tiger" and perform the YMCA dance as crewmembers pelt you with water balloons and mock you over loudspeakers—all while you're bouncing across the water at speeds faster than forty-five miles per hour, courtesy of the boat's two 2,600-horsepower engines. In order to limit its liability, the tour explicitly bars pregnant women from riding on the *Beast*. But regardless of whether or not you are carrying a child, I'd recommend skipping the speedboat and taking the Staten Island Ferry instead. It gives great views of the Statue of Liberty, has ample deck space to perform the 1970s dance sensations of your choosing, and, unlike most things in New York, it's free.

31 THE GROVER CLEVELAND SERVICE AREA

I'd actually recommend not seeing *any* of the rest stops along the New Jersey Turnpike, each of which is named for a notable person who was born or lived in the state. The Thomas Edison Starbucks, the James Fenimore Cooper Burger King—call me un-

American, but I think there's something inherently depressing about Walt Whitman being commemorated by a Cinnabon franchise.

According to *Looking for America on the New Jersey Turnpike*—which itself might qualify as a *Book Not to Read Before You Die*—several rest stops have reputations that go beyond just convenient places to grab a cup of coffee. The Vince Lombardi area was once known as a hot spot for cruising gay men; anecdotal reports suggest that the Joyce Kilmer service area used to be frequented by prostitutes (they've now been supplanted by a Sbarro).

Graced with branches of Popeye's, Pizza Hut Express, and, in the case of Woodrow Wilson, a Blimpie, what does impress me about these rest stops is their ambition; it's hard, after all, to build a service area that really captures the essence of Alexander Hamilton. But with a Roy Rogers *and* a Carvel, no one can say they didn't try.

32 THE ROOM WHERE SPAM SUBJECT LINES ARE CREATED

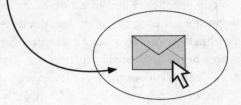

The subject lines for spam are probably the product of some electronic word scrambler, but I like to think that they are the brainchildren of a secret society of perverts. I imagine these men meeting in a subterranean room someplace in the former Soviet Union, flipping through stacks of porn as they toss ideas back and forth about what tagline is most likely to boost illicit Viagra sales.

"Your dick will explode!" shouts a chubby bald man, looking up from his favorite teenage centerfold.

"Too literal. I like 'Nasty anal fruit salad,'" says another, fingers poised above his computer's sticky keyboard.

"How about 'Put your horse in my pussy'?" suggests a man at the front of the room. Well respected by his peers, he is known for his use of metaphor, most recently in a campaign titled "Power up your meat cigar."

"I think we're going for something more along the lines of 'Knock down trees with your GIANT COCK,'" responds a bespectacled man. "We don't want to confuse people."

Before he can elaborate a short man jumps out of the shadows—the resident surrealist. "Hamburgler orgasms!" he shouts. "Ascent tampon! Dong toast!"

After a brief masturbation break, the men debate suggestions ranging from the religious ("I've got a twelve-inch rabbi") to the seasonal ("What's new in summer? Testicles"). Eventually they settle on a polite inquiry—"I HUMBLY REQUEST FOR YOUR ASS."

And then, as they prepare for a celebratory dong toast, the leader of the group hits "send."

33 ANYWHERE WRITTEN ABOUT BY NICK KRISTOF

Nick Kristof, the two-time Pullitzer Prize–winning columnist for the *New York Times*, gravitates toward subjects most people don't want to think about. Rape victims in Pakistan, dying mothers in West Africa, slum dwellers in Haiti—if a story says "human tragedy," Kristof will find it. Through his columns, blog, books, and videos, he encourages people to pay attention to atrocities so awful that they're tempting to ignore.

This is a great public service, but it doesn't mean you should allow Kristof to plan your next family vacation. "He's . . . one of the very few Americans to be at least a two-time visitor to every member of the Axis of Evil," says his *Times* bio. "During his travels, he has had unpleasant experiences with malaria, mobs and an African airplane crash." In a column of tips for student travelers, he skips standard advice ("Bring earplugs!") and heads straight for the nitty-gritty: "If you are held up by bandits with large guns, shake hands respectfully with each of your persecutors," he writes. "It's very important to be polite to people who might kill you."

On the upside, though, Kristof definitely knows how to avoid tourist traps. And he's not one for crappy souvenirs. Whereas most people blow their vacation budgets on booze and tacky T-shirts, Kristof puts his money toward more worthy causes: he once celebrated a trip to Cambodia by buying two teenagers out of slavery.

✕✕✕✕ NICK KRISTOF ✕✕✕✕

Experiences That Nick Kristof Does Not Think Are Worth Having Before You Die

- Being stuck at a small airport in Xishuangbanna, China, soon after it opened to foreigners. With the entire town watching, the security guard searches my bag, finds my deodorant—and asks what it is. As a fascinated crowd of several hundred people listens attentively, I try to explain that Westerners use this to avoid stinking.

- Sitting trapped in a small UN-chartered plane as it is preparing to crash-land in the Democratic Republic of the Congo in the middle of the civil war. On the bright side, I have my laptop and satellite phone, and am trying to buy life insurance.

- Standing in a no-man's-land at night in Lebanon as an unidentified militia points guns at us and asks me and my friend our identities. My friend says "Australia," in a thick Australian accent. The gunman gets excited. He double checks: "You say, 'Israel'?"

NICK KRISTOF is a Pulitzer Prize–winning *New York Times* columnist.

✕✕✕✕

THE TOKYO SUMMERLAND WAVE POOL, AUGUST 14, 2007, 3 P.M.

There are times when a picture really is worth a thousand words. Like this one—a photograph of the Tokyo Summerland Wave Pool taken during the Japanese festival of Obon. Technically Obon is a time to commemorate the dead, but apparently

it can also be an invitation to grab your water wings and head to the pool.

According to photographer Michael Keferl, this shot was taken shortly after the wave pool reopened (it had been closed for repair)—and no, it wasn't Photoshopped. These revelers just take their wave pools seriously. They don't have time for you and your silly concerns, like how a lifeguard would be able to rescue you from the crush, or what you should do if the guy next to you starts peeing. They just want to know the answer to one question: how can I squeeze my pink inner tube into that pool?

As one commenter put it, the resulting scene combines the "acoustics of a high school gymnasium with the ambiance of being bathed in lukewarm urine." It also raises that age-old philosophical question: if a small child gets pulled underwater but everyone is having too much fun to notice, did she really drown?

35 MID-JANUARY IN WHITTIER, ALASKA

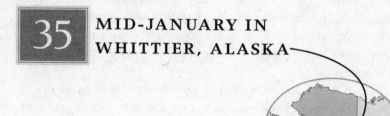

Cut off from the rest of Alaska by thirty-five-hundred-foot-tall mountains, covered for most of the year by heavy clouds, the town of Whittier, Alaska, might not exist if it weren't for World War II. After the Japanese bombed the Aleutian Islands in 1942, the U.S. Army wanted to find a place in Alaska to build a secret military installation—ideally an isolated spot with an ice-free port and bad weather that would make it harder to see from the air. Tucked into the northeast corner of the Kenai Peninsula and cut off from the mainland by the Chugach Mountains, Whittier qualified on all counts.

After deciding on a location, the army's first task was to build a tunnel. So it began blasting through the granite, and by 1943 had completed a 2.5-mile passageway to Whittier that, until recently, was open only to trains. Next, it built two huge apartment buildings to house the residents of the town.

At its peak in 1960, Whittier's population was about twelve hundred, but that didn't last long. When the army pulled out of Whittier, its population dropped to a mere eighty Whittiots, which meant that when the 1964 Good Friday Earthquake killed thirteen people, it wiped out a considerable percentage of the town's population. As of 2007, Whittier was back up to a whopping 174 residents, but with more people migrating out than coming in, it's unlikely to ever reach its former peak.

Part of the reason Whittier has never been heavily populated is that until the tunnel was opened to cars, the only way to get there was by sea or rail. Even today, the one-lane tunnel can only accommodate one direction of traffic at a time, and has to alternate between trains and cars. Add in daily maintenance periods and there are times when you can wait more than two hours for the chance to pay the $12 toll.

Of course, this only applies when the tunnel is *open*. It closes each evening around 11, so don't linger too long if you intend to make it back to Anchorage for the night. What's more, on April 11, 2009, a large rockslide tumbled onto the highway leading to the tunnel. It was shut down entirely for more than a month, stranding many of the town's residents and giving new relevancy to the POW—PRISONER

Begich Towers, the town's only apartment building—and home to most of Whittier's residents

OF WHITTIER—T-shirts that were popular before the tunnel opened to cars.

Whittier does have a beautiful hiking trail and great wildlife, but be sure to time your visit well—it receives no direct sunlight from November to February and gets more than twenty feet of snow per year.

36 ONONDAGA LAKE

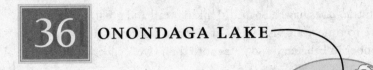

United States   New York

The 1400s were good to Onondaga Lake, a 4.6-square-mile lake that sits northwest of Syracuse, New York. Back then, it enjoyed a privileged status at the heart of the Iroquois Confederacy. Its halcyon days lasted until the nineteenth century, when it became a popular holiday destination, ringed with resorts and restaurants featuring locally caught fish. But once industrial development in Syracuse really kicked in, the lake got screwed.

First was the sewage: as the nearby city of Syracuse grew, its planners designed its water system to discharge the city's domestic and industrial waste directly into the lake.

Then came the Solvay Process Company, a soda ash producer that opened on Onondaga's western shore in 1884 and proceeded to release millions of gallons of by-products into the lake per day. That got rid of the company's trash—but it also killed off most of the cold-water fish.

Pollution eventually forced the resorts and beaches to close—at which point you'd think someone would have realized that using the lake as a garbage can was a bad idea. But instead, Solvay was replaced by the Allied Chemical and Dye Company, which discharged about 165,000 pounds of mercury into the water over the next fifteen years.

Other companies followed Allied's lead, dumping chemicals like polychlorinated biphenyls (PCBs) and chlorinated benzene into the mix.

It was only after the Clean Water Act passed in 1972 that people started trying to clean up Onondaga. The sewage treatment plant was updated; several of the heaviest polluters were shut down. But unfortunately, these efforts came late—almost forty years later, the lake is still unsafe to swim in, and the sediments at its bottom are on the federal Superfund list. A group called the Onondaga Lake Partnership has made admirable progress toward making Onondaga Lake a safe environment for fish and other marine life. But considering the lake's remaining problems, like large plumes of algae and overflows of untreated sewage, it's going to be a while before you see me doing laps.

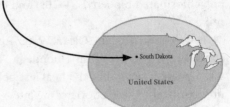

• South Dakota

United States

B eautiful though it may be, South Dakota doesn't have much in the way of manmade attractions. But what it lacks in number, it makes up in scale—the presidential portraits on Mount Rushmore, carved into the face of a mountain, are each over sixty feet tall.

Peering out from the mountain, the oversize faces of George Washington, Thomas Jefferson, Abraham Lincoln, and Theodore Roosevelt were designed to celebrate the first 150 years of American history. With America more than 230 years old and going (relatively) strong, Mount Rushmore still draws millions of visitors per year.

That's the part I don't get, because while Mount Rushmore is an impressive achievement, it's really not that interesting. There's no jackalope or fake Tyrannosaurus Rex (see Wall Drug, p. 42); in fact, three of the people featured in the sculpture also appear on the bills you'll be using to pay the park entrance fee. Take into account the fact that the sculptures were carved into hills considered sacred to the Lakota Sioux, and it starts seeming less like a testament to the American spirit and more like an example of us acting like jerks.

But what really confuses me is the lack of creativity. Unlike many other historical sites, Mount Rushmore never had a purpose besides being a tourist attraction: it was built specifically to draw visitors to South Dakota's Black Hills. So why not spice things up a bit? Mountaineering guides could lead climbing expeditions up Thomas Jefferson's nose. An entrepreneurial company could rig a zip line from Teddy Roosevelt's mustache. Each summer Mount Rushmore does offer sculpting classes, but still. Gazing up at the possibility that is Washington's forehead, I can't help but think we could do a little better.

38 AMATEUR NIGHT AT A SHOOTING RANGE

I f I'm going to spend an evening shooting guns, I want there to be plenty of adult supervision—especially if half the clientele has never fired one before.

This was not the case at Jackson Arms Shooting Range in southern San Francisco where I attended a handgun-themed bachelor party with a bunch of other firearm neophytes. Housed in what looked like an industrial warehouse, the parking lot was full of pickup trucks with bumper stickers not typically associated with the San Francisco Bay Area, and the walls of the lobby and gift shop were lined with rifles. When my husband jokingly asked whether the shop had ever been held up, our teacher didn't smile. "No," he said. "We're all holstered."

Holstered he was—when he led our group into a back classroom, I noticed the butts of twin handguns protruding from under his T-shirt. I'd hoped that the fact that he was carrying at least two firearms would mean that he would have a very hands-on approach to teaching us how to use them. But instead, he treated our gun education with the gravitas one might find at an employee training session for a fast-food restaurant.

"What's this?" the teacher asked, pointing at the back of the room.

"A wall," someone responded.

"No. The men's bathroom. Bullets go through walls." He appeared pleased at this punchline. "Never point your gun at anything other than the target."

This was good advice, but I wanted more. I wanted to know how the safety worked, and how to tell if it was on. I wanted to know what to do if the bullets jammed, and where the location of the emergency exits were, just in case the person next to me freaked out.

Instead, the teacher gave a quick demonstration of how to load the bullets, and explained how to aim ("Point it toward your target"). Then he handed us plastic caddies filled with handguns and boxes of bullets and let us loose in the firing range, a large concrete room divided into lanes. It looked like a cross between a parking lot and a bowling alley, with one important difference: everyone in it was armed.

Much to my distress, these guns were not tethered to anything, which meant that there was no way to prevent a fellow guest from turning toward you and shooting you in the face. This would not have been such an issue if we had been the only people in the room, but we weren't. A group of twenty-something men gathered in a lane near us, all jockeying for a chance to shoot. Several loners lurked nearby, making me question whether a violent criminal really would have bothered to tick the box next to PRIOR FELONIES when filling out his liability form. But most frightening of all was a woman standing in the next lane, forty-something years old with dyed blond hair. Wearing a pink T-shirt and glasses that had a line of masking tape across the lenses to help steady her sight, she was taking slow, methodical shots with a .45-caliber handgun—not at a bull's eye, but at the outline of a man's torso.

39 CIUDAD JUÁREZ

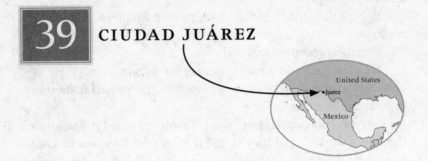

"What is it about borders? Why are they inherently exhilarating?" asked the *New York Times* in December 2006 in an article about El Paso, Texas, and Ciudad Juárez, Mexico, two adjacent cities on opposite sides of the Rio Grande. Its focus was food, but in recent years Juárez has become best known for crime: between January 2008 and early 2009, more than eighteen hundred people were murdered.

The majority of these killings are attributed to drug cartels, but there's a more systemic problem. The Mexican army is in the midst of an aggressive military effort against the cartels, but its soldiers have also been accused of abusing local police offers. In turn, the police force itself tortures detainees and indulges in other horrific abuse: one woman, a former beauty queen, was allegedly held for three days and repeatedly raped by eight policemen. And then there are the drug cartels themselves. Responsible for public assassinations, gruesome decapitations, and the murders of innocent citizens, they're waging a bloody fight against one another and anyone who stands in their way.

What's particularly terrifying about this battle is that many of Juárez's victims have little or no connection to the battles raging around them. Innocent people have been shot in broad daylight; in the city of 1.6 million people, there were 17,000 car thefts and 1,650 carjackings in 2008 alone. The U.S. State Department warns that "recent Mexican army and police confrontations with drug cartels have resembled small-unit combat, with cartels employing automatic weapons and grenades" and says that Juárez has become subject to "public shootouts during daylight hours in shopping centers and other public venues." It recommends staying close to tourist sites, traveling only during the day, using toll roads wherever possible, avoiding ATMs, and, for women in particular, not traveling alone.

The border is indeed exhilarating—but unfortunately for anyone trying to live or visit Ciudad Juárez, not in a good way.

40 THE WORLD'S SKINNIEST BUILDINGS

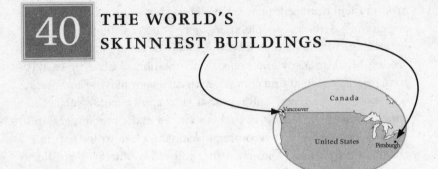

Some fights are hard to get worked up about—like the spat between the Sam Kee Building in Vancouver, British Columbia, and the so-called Skinny Building in Pittsburgh, Pennsylvania, over which structure is the thinnest.

At four feet eleven inches at its base (and six feet on its second story, thanks to bay windows), the Sam Kee Building has been named the skinniest commercial building in the world by both the *Guinness Book of World Records* and Ripley's Believe It or Not! Like many other slender buildings, it was built partially out of spite: its lot, originally a normal size, got reduced by twenty-four feet when Vancouver expropriated the space to widen Pender Street in 1912. Designed in 1913, the building's basement actually extends underneath the sidewalk and used to house the only public baths in Vancouver's Chinatown (not to mention an escape tunnel for nearby opium dens); the upper two stories were devoted to shops and very narrow apartments.

But watch out, Mr. Kee—Pittsburgh's Skinny Building wants to challenge its claim to be the thinnest commercial space in the world. At five feet two inches wide from top to bottom, the Skinny Building is indeed more consistently emaciated than the top-heavy Sam Kee. What's more, at three stories tall, it's a floor higher. Back in the early 2000s, Pat Clark and Al Kovacik—a consultant and architect who were leasing the top two floors of the Skinny Building as an arts venue, sent photographs to Vancouver's visitors' center as proof that their building was narrower.

Clark and Kovacik may have had a point, but unfortunately, their argument may now be moot—in 2007, their landlord refused to renew their lease, and the arts venue was forced to close. With that attraction gone, the building's main draw is purely its diminutive size, which, as anyone who knows someone obsessed with their weight can attest, is really not that interesting.

41 THE GREAT PACIFIC GARBAGE PATCH

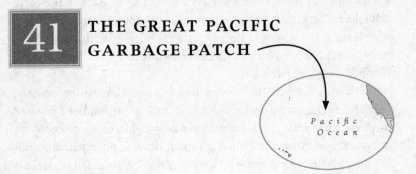

Pacific Ocean

Also known as the Eastern Garbage Patch or the Pacific Trash Vortex, the Great Pacific Garbage Patch is a huge, swirling mass of plastic in the middle of the ocean that's been estimated to be twice the size of Texas.

The garbage patch—if one hundred million tons of debris can be called a patch—was discovered in 1997 by a Californian sailor, oceanographer, and furniture restorer named Charles Moore, who decided to take a shortcut on his way back from a sailing competition in Hawaii. He and his crew sailed their fifty-foot catamaran through the North Pacific Subtropical Gyre—an area usually avoided by sailors because of its lack of wind—and were shocked to find themselves navigating through what appeared to be an endless sea of plastic.

Bottle caps, Legos, flip-flops, toothbrushes, Styrofoam cups, footballs, even entire kayaks—Moore had accidentally guided his boat into the final resting place for an incomprehensible amount of plastic trash, pieces of which were close to half a century old. Intrigued and horrified, Moore returned on a research trip two years later and discovered that the patch extended some thirty feet underwater, with increasingly tiny pieces of plastic swirling in the ocean like multi-colored fish food. (Since no microbes exist that can digest plastic, it doesn't biodegrade; instead, exposure to sunlight and currents breaks its polymer chains into smaller and smaller pieces.) In parts, the water of the patch contained six times more plastic than it did plankton—a ratio that has since dramatically increased.

Moore brought himself out of retirement to found the Algalita Marine Research Foundation, which is devoted to studying the composition and effects of this giant mass of plastic. This isn't the cheeriest research assignment; Algalita's research assignments include examining the stomach contents of dead albatrosses (the United Nations Environment Programme estimates that plastic debris kills more than a million seabirds a year) and investigating how, exactly, the toxicants in plastic dissolve into ocean water. Among the disturbing facts they've discovered: a lot of the plastic trash is from nurdles—lentil-size pellets of raw plastic that are used in manufacturing and frequently escape into the water. Also, plastic has an unfortunate tendency to act as a chemical sponge for other toxicants, like hydrocarbons and DDT, which nurdle-nibbling fish can pass up the food chain to our dinner plates.

So why not just clean it up? According to the folks at Algalita, that would be completely impossible: not only is the patch miles wide and at least 30 feet deep, but it's less a plastic island than a plastic soup, full of tiny particles that can't be recovered without scooping up plankton and other marine life at the same time. Even worse, since much of the plastic is so tiny and/or transparent that it doesn't show up in satellite images, no one yet knows how much of the world's oceans have been contaminated.

The Customs Office
at the Buenos Aires Airport

It would not be quite true to say that the package containing my all-weather jacket for Tierra del Fuego arrived safely in Buenos Aires. Rather, in this country that suggests all was not lost when the Soviet Union dissolved, I—with visions of packages dancing in my head—got to my mailing address only to find a sheaf of stapled papers with, on top, a long letter addressed to *estimado cliente.* "Esteemed client," it said, "call these number between 10 and 3 or these numbers from 9 to 1 and 2 to 5, and then . . ."

So I called my excellent cousin Bernardo, a native of Buenos Aires, who later told me that when his wife heard I had to deal with customs, she said something akin to "oh my God," or "the Lord preserve us," or some such locution. We drove across town from Bernardo's business at about 2 P.M. via the lawless, jammed-up surface streets—there are very few stop signs and not so many lanes or traffic lights in the Darwinist traffic here—and then the long straightaway with the innumerable tolls of about 17 cents apiece to the international airport. Bernardo asked a few dozen people to initiate us into the secret of the location, and we stashed the car in a nonsecured parking lot and asked some more people for directions, some of whom also needed to look at my passport, and so we arrived at the secret customs hell.

Bernardo talked en route about the endless corruption of this country's government, from the airline that was supposed to be de-privatized and turned out to be run by part of the president's family, which was shipping suitcases of cocaine on passenger-less passenger planes to Spain, to the congressional aide who suggested that, for a sum of money, the law affecting his business could be rearranged. So, to customs: a corridor in a warehouse looking into three air-conditioned cubicle-like offices. We went into the first cubicle and got some papers stamped so we could stand in the line of anxious, frustrated people for an hour or so in the extraordinary heat, not knowing if our turn would ever come before the office shut in a mere two and a half hours.

Waiting, waiting, waiting, and then finally the appointment in office two, with the young woman with badly dyed hair and forms that must be filled out, but whose government copies would only be tossed in a loose pile, suggesting no one would ever look at them again or even be able to find anything in them (in this country that still uses carbon paper). And then to office three, where we got some more papers and rubber stamps, showed my passport some more, and then, as though it were all an elaborate dance, a few more rotations: the melancholic official walked us to the actual parcel site where we jointly viewed my parcel's contents to prove they were not new or valuable, and it was then sealed up again against theft by the officials with tape that was the equivalent of official seals so we could go back to office two to get another round of stamps and then back to office one to pay a toll of 43.5 pesos, about $14, and then, with the man from office three, we walked back to office four and actually received the damn thing. I thought of the funky technology and endless bureaucracy in the movie *Brazil*, the labyrinths people get stuck in, the rumpled piles of documents, and the guerrilla repairman who cuts through bureaucratic red tape to make things actually work. It was clear that though the normative purpose of data collection is data retrieval or the ability to track, these three offices with their loose piles of documents have nothing to do with any such thing. And that without a skilled local, I would've never seen my Tierra del Fuego gear again.

REBECCA SOLNIT is the author of *A Paradise Built in Hell: The Extraordinary Communities That Arise in Disaster.*

✕✕✕✕

42   ANY HOTEL THAT USED TO BE A PRISON

There are many contenders for the world's least pleasant hotels—dasparkhotel in Austria puts guests up in drainpipes, for example, and the Null Stern Hotel (German for "zero star") offers rooms in a Swiss nuclear bomb shelter. But Karostas Cietums in Latvia tops the list. A Soviet-era military prison, it was in active use till 1997, and boasts that ever since the first years of its existence, "it has been a place to break people's lives and suppress their free will." Sign me up for the honeymoon suite.

The prison's original clientele was a diverse group of convicts, ranging from members of the tsarist army and deserters of the German Wehrmacht to men judged by Stalin's government to be enemies of the people. These days, it caters to guests who are attracted to the idea of spending the night in a place where, according to the hotel's promotional material, more than 150 people have been shot.

Unsurprisingly, accommodations are sparse; rates include iron beds and authentic prison meals, and lucky children can spend a night in prison bunks. But threadbare mattresses are far from the only attractions: in the museum, you'll have an opportunity to try on a gas mask or buy vintage souvenirs, like former inmates' aluminum spoons. Other options include participating in an ominous-sounding "surprise tour" and an evening activity that gives guests the chance to "live the part of a prisoner on a dismal night." Most activities require participants to apply in advance and sign what's referred to as "the Agreement," which states, among other things, that "Participants may receive insulting instructions and orders which must be carried out without objection" and that "In case of disobedience prisoners may be punished."

43 THE TOP OF MOUNT WASHINGTON IN A SNOWSTORM

The warnings on the trails up Mount Washington don't mince words. STOP they say. THE AREA AHEAD HAS THE WORST WEATHER IN AMERICA. MANY HAVE DIED THERE FROM EXPOSURE, EVEN IN THE SUMMER. TURN BACK NOW IF THE WEATHER IS BAD.

It's hard to objectively define worst weather, but by most people's standards, the top of Mount Washington would qualify. At 6,288 feet, the New Hampshire mountain is small in comparison to the United States' western peaks, but its location at the convergence of several storm tracks, not to mention its height and north-south orientation, means that it gets hit with hurricane-force winds and snowstorms all year round. Not only does Mount Washington's summit hold the record for the world's strongest recorded wind speed—231 miles per hour—but its average yearly temperature is only 27.2 degrees.

Despite its weather conditions, Mount Washington draws a steady stream of tourists—most of whom define conquering the summit as buying a bumper sticker that says THIS CAR CLIMBED MT. WASHINGTON. But hard-core hikers also tackle the mountain by foot, and occasionally they never make it down—more than one hundred people have perished on its slopes.

If you're unfortunate enough to find yourself on Mount Washington during a winter storm and can't find shelter, you're probably going to die. But at least you'll have something pretty to look at: rime ice, a feathery frosting that's beloved by nature photographers. When a storm hits, these delicate ice structures will begin to build up on rocks, trees, and, if you wait long enough, your body. Your hands may be too numb to reach for your camera, but at least you can take comfort in knowing that your last vision will be one of which Ansel Adams would have approved.

44 THE BOTTOM OF THE KOLA SUPERDEEP BOREHOLE

Everyone knows about the U.S.-Soviet Space Race of the 1960s. But few people are aware that at the same time the two countries were vying to hurl manned spacecraft into orbit, they were also sprinting in the opposite direction: toward the earth's core.

Or, to be more specific, toward something called the Mohorovičić Discontinuity, thought to be the boundary between the earth's crust and its magma-filled mantle. America was the first to try—in 1957 it launched Project Mohole, a later-abandoned plan to reach the so-called Moho by drilling through the ocean floor. Distracted by a different, equally important project—launching the first dog into orbit—the Soviets didn't get started on their own Project Moho till 1962, and started drilling in 1970. But while they may have lost that first battle, the Soviets won the war: at more than seven miles deep, the Kola Superdeep Borehole is the deepest hole in the world.

Why were the two countries racing toward this particular goal? At first, the answer seemed to be: why not? I mean, dude. It's the world's *deepest hole.*

But there were also scientific reasons, and as the Soviet team drilled (and drilled and drilled), taking core samples along the way, its members discovered everything from unexpected water to fossils some four miles underground. They also disproved their own assumptions about how quickly things heat up: by the time they reached their stopping point, the rock was so hot that it was malleable, flowing closed whenever the scientists replaced the drill bit. In order to continue, the project would have required new heat-resistant technology and massive renovations to its equipment.

Unfortunately, official interest in the hole had waned in the twenty-four years since the project began. And so, much to the chagrin of workers who had spent two decades in a remote outpost boring a hole into rock, drilling stopped in 1994, just 1.7 miles short of the goal.

These days the hole's core samples—the last of which was estimated to be over 2.7 billion years old—are housed about six miles south of the drilling site. But to people not acquainted with the works of Russia's State Scientific Enterprise on Superdeep Drilling and Complex Investigations in the Earth's Interior, the hole is basically unknown. Which, when it comes to would-be visitors, might be a good thing—the Kola Superdeep Borehole is only about nine inches wide.

45 THE INSIDE OF A dB DRAG RACER DURING COMPETITION

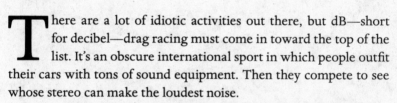

There are a lot of idiotic activities out there, but dB—short for decibel—drag racing must come in toward the top of the list. It's an obscure international sport in which people outfit their cars with tons of sound equipment. Then they compete to see whose stereo can make the loudest noise.

When I say tons, I mean it literally: one dB drag racer profiled by *Popular Science* was the proud owner of an eighteen-year-old Dodge Caravan that weighed ten thousand pounds. Too heavy to drive, too cramped to carry a passenger, the car's sole purpose was to make a 74 Hz sound—known in the dB drag racing world as a "burp"—as loudly as possible.

Competitors soup up their cars in all sorts of ways. To increase sound pressure inside the car, which in turn raises the intensity of the noise, racers bolt the doors shut and fill them with concrete. They replace the windows with Plexiglas—many of the burps are loud enough to shatter glass. During competition, teammates gather around the car and push against it from all sides, sometimes lying spread eagle on the roof to try to increase pressure at the moment of the burp. The resulting noise is what the writer from *Popular Science* described as "what you hear when you inadvertently turn your home stereo on with the volume all the way up and a loose speaker wire: a rattling, destructive, marrow-fluttering hum."

So far the world record is 180.5 dB, achieved in 2007 in a concrete-filled Volvo. To give you a sense of how loud that is, a 747 jet emits about 140 dB at takeoff, and every 10 dB increase represents a doubling of noise. But who really cares about the specific number of decibels produced? Were you to be stupid enough to shove aside the amps and subwoofers and sit inside a car during competition, that eardrum-bursting burp would probably be the last sound you'd ever hear.

46 SHANGRI-LA

China

• Sichuan

• Tibet

• Zhongdian

• Bhutan

Tucked into a hidden valley in the Himalayas and watched over by a Tibetan lamasery, Shangri-La is supposed to be paradise: a place where everyone is permanently happy and no one ever grows old.

Only problem is it's imaginary. Our Western notions of Shangri-La come from the 1933 novel *Lost Horizon* by James Hilton, in which a British diplomat named Hugh Conway happens upon it when he survives a plane crash in the Tibetan mountains. After discovering that this remote lamasery comes complete with hot water, central heating, and a fetching young Manchu woman named Lo-Tsen, he decides to stay awhile.

Hilton's novel didn't get much attention until he published his best-known work, *Goodbye, Mr. Chips*, but it then became a bestseller. The mythical land so captured the American imagination that for a brief period of time, Franklin Delano Roosevelt renamed the presidential retreat Shangri-La in its honor. In 1956 it even inspired an unsuccessful Broadway musical.

Entrepreneurs have been trying to co-opt Shangri-La ever since the success of Conway's novel. In 2001, the Chinese county of Zhongdian officially renamed itself Shangri-La in an attempt to lure tourists; there's a Shangri-La resort in Northern Pakistan's Skardu Valley, and a worldwide Shangri-La hotel chain. But no one's really sure where the actual inspiration for Shangri-La is located. Maybe it's in Sichuan Province. Or the Yarlung Tsangpo Canyon. Or, for that matter, Bhutan.

Regardless of what place Hilton was thinking of, the myth on which Shangri-La is based far predates *Lost Horizon*. It's thought to be related to the legend of Shambala, a hidden kingdom in the mountains of Tibet where all the residents were peaceful and happy, living in what some say was a state of enlightenment. This myth may have been based on the ancient city of Tsaparang or a civilization called Shang Shung—it depends on which trekker you speak to. Regardless, would-be visitors beware: traveling to either spot requires a long journey at high altitudes and a large budget for pack mules.

An easier option is the Shangri-La in Orange, Texas. The creation of a philanthropist named H. J. Lutcher Stark, it's an enormous nature preserve highlighting Stark's favorite flower, the azalea. Opened to the public in 1946, it was a favorite vacation destination for over a decade until a major snowstorm hit East Texas in 1958 and destroyed much of the park. Recently reopened, the Texan Shangri-La might not be able to promise eternal life or happiness, but at least it has a really nice garden.

I f you like fields full of rotting corpses, visit a body farm. Technically called "forensic anthropology facilities," they're outdoor sites devoted to the study of how human bodies decompose. Strewn with partially rotted bodies, they could also be mistaken as sets for horror movies.

Why would anyone want to watch a body being eaten by maggots? To help solve crimes, of course. By studying how bodies decompose in a variety of circumstances (buried, unburied, underwater, in the trunk of a car), forensic anthropologists are better able to reconstruct the causes of death.

Luckily for the squeamish, there are only three body farms in the United States. The oldest, in Tennessee, was founded in 1971 by a scientist named Dr. William Bass. Police kept asking for his help analyzing bodies in criminal cases, and he figured that in order to answer their questions, he needed a better understanding of how corpses disintegrate. That meant getting a body, putting it outside, and watching what happened next.

Dr. Bass's original facility could only accommodate one person, and most of his corpses were unclaimed bodies obtained through the medical examiner's office. But these days the farm is a three-acre complex with enough room for up to forty bodies at a time. If you're interested in the full experience, the facility has even launched a donation program so that you can bequeath your corpse to the cause.

Crime shows like *CSI* have glamorized the field of forensic anthropology, but the reality of a body farm is, to put it bluntly, revolting. Tissues begin to release a green substance; lungs leak liquid through corpses' mouths and noses. "Truly, this work is not for the faint of heart," researchers at the University of Tennessee warn would-be forensic anthropologists. "Rotten smells, decomposing flesh, maggots, and body fluids are everyday occurrences, and you will be elbow deep in them."

Unfortunately, they're not being figurative.

48 AN AA MEETING WHEN YOU'RE DRUNK

This is not one of the twelve steps.

JUPITER'S WORST MOON

At ten thousand degrees Fahrenheit, the sun is a strong candidate for the worst vacation destination in space. So are black holes. Not only do they suck up and destroy everything around them, explained an astronomer whom I asked to select some of space's worst spots, but they'll tear you apart atom by atom—a process that sounds even worse when you realize that black holes can slow down time. We considered Venus (750 degrees Fahrenheit and surrounded by clouds of sulfuric acid); we thought about deep space ("great for those worried about a hectic itinerary").

But the eventual winner was Io, one of Jupiter's four main moons.

With a mottled surface covered in splotches of orange, yellow, red, and dark brown, Io is said to look like a pizza, but I think it more closely resembles a rotten orange. You could also skip all food analogies and compare Io directly to hell.

The most volcanic known object in the solar system, Io has over four hundred volcanoes, which spew sulfuric plumes up to 310 miles high. Its surface is covered with flowing lava and giant calderas. And yet, ironically, it's also freezing: volcanoes are the only source of heat on a planet that routinely reaches −230 degrees Fahrenheit.

Io does offer fantastic views of Jupiter, but the beauty is offset by the fact that Io is bathed in sulfur dioxide, which would fill your last gasps with an overwhelming stench of rotten eggs. Io has no native water, but if its volcanic gases got into the liquid in your Nalgene, you'd be drinking sulfuric acid. And while Io's low gravity would make it a hit with the kids, their enjoyment would be short-lived—nighttime temperatures are so cold that at the end of every forty-two-hour day, the atmosphere collapses.

Io and Jupiter

✗✗✗✗ J. MAARTEN TROOST ✗✗✗✗

Splitting the Czech

O ne morning in southern Turkey, in the vicinity of Bodrum and the sun-dappled waters of the Aegean Sea, I fell over a waterfall. I hadn't intended to do this, of course. Nowhere on my itinerary did it say FALL OVER WATERFALL. Languid swims, yes. Edifying hikes up to the ruins of the ancients, sure. Fall over waterfall, no.

But fall over I did. I would like to think that in that terrifying moment when I lost my footing—that awful instant when I merged with a stream that rushed inexorably toward an unknown abyss—that time slowed down. Perhaps I had a moment to ruminate and ponder the admonitions of my guide. "Don't climb up there," he'd said moments earlier. "Last month, two men died climbing above the waterfall." Where were they from, I'd asked. "They were Czech." I'm only half Czech, I'd said. Ha ha. No problem.

Alas, I have no memory of my thoughts as I hurtled toward the lip of the falls. I'm told I screamed, so they were presumably not happy thoughts. And it's no wonder, really. It's endless all the ways water, rocks, and gravity can conspire to hurt you (three fractured vertebrae, shattered feet, concussion, lacerations, in my case). But since then, no matter how unpleasant the travel experience, I've always managed to look at the sunny side of things. I'm alive. I'm still walking. And I'm only half Czech.

J. MAARTEN TROOST is the author of *Lost on Planet China: The Strange and True Story of One Man's Attempt to Understand the World's Most Mystifying Nation or How He Became Comfortable Eating Live Squid.*

✗✗✗✗

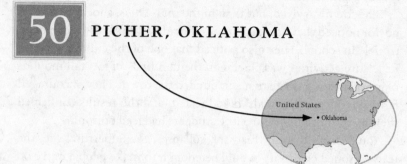

50 PICHER, OKLAHOMA

United States

• Oklahoma

As a vacation destination, Picher, Oklahoma, has one thing going for it: privacy. Come for the weekend and you'll likely be the only person there—the government paid everyone else to leave.

That's because the town, which was once home to about sixteen thousand people, sits on top of huge deposits of lead and zinc. Its mines yielded nearly five hundred thousand tons of ore in 1925 alone, and metal from Picher was used for bullets in both World Wars.

But after World War II ended, Picher began to collapse. Literally. Thanks to huge natural and manmade caverns beneath the town, its main street was fenced off in the 1950s for fear that it would cave in, and in 1967, nine homes sank into an abandoned part of the mine.

Things went downhill from there. After the last of Picher's mines closed in the 1970s, a local rancher noticed orange spots on the coats of his white horses. He followed them to the field and discovered that the water in nearby Tar Creek was orange from acidic liquids seeping up from the abandoned mines; it turned out to have such high levels of heavy metals that in 1983, Picher was named as one of America's first Superfund sites.

The town survived, but then in the mid–1990s, a local nurse and doctor noticed that a suspicious number of Picher's kids were having trouble in school. They also noticed that one of the children's favorite leisure activities was playing in the hundreds-of-feet-tall mounds of gravel mining waste that surrounded the town. They encouraged families to have their kids' blood tested, and the results confirmed their fears: more than 190 of the students had lead poisoning.

You'd think that all this—the collapses, the Superfund site, the lead-poisoned children—would be enough to make people move on their own. But when the federal government launched its buyout of Picher in 2006, motivated by a report showing that an even more substantial area of the town was at risk of collapse, a surprising number of residents refused to leave.

But fate had it in for Picher. On May 10, 2008, a devastating tornado hit the town, killing at least six people and destroying about half of Picher's remaining homes. It was the last straw. Now devoid of residents, Picher's only remaining attractions are its dilapidated buildings, its infamous orange creek, and a swamp filled with floating tires.

51 TIERRA SANTA THEME PARK

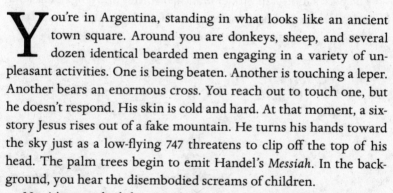

Y ou're in Argentina, standing in what looks like an ancient town square. Around you are donkeys, sheep, and several dozen identical bearded men engaging in a variety of unpleasant activities. One is being beaten. Another is touching a leper. Another bears an enormous cross. You reach out to touch one, but he doesn't respond. His skin is cold and hard. At that moment, a six-story Jesus rises out of a fake mountain. He turns his hands toward the sky just as a low-flying 747 threatens to clip off the top of his head. The palm trees begin to emit Handel's *Messiah*. In the background, you hear the disembodied screams of children.

No, it's not a bad dream. It's Tierra Santa in Buenos Aires, one of the world's most popular theme parks devoted to the Holy Land. Located next to a family-friendly water park and a major airport, it boasts one of the only crucifixes to be backed by a waterslide.

Since the park was designed by a renowned plastic artist, the majority of its animals aren't alive. Neither are the palm trees, the beggars, or, for that matter, the whores. (The belly dancers are a different story.) This abundance of plastic will become especially noticeable when you are ushered into the park's first exhibit, El Pesebre, in which robotic plastic figurines act out the nativity in what's billed as "the world's largest manger." Occasionally technical difficulties delay Jesus's birth, but since Mary goes into labor approximately once every half hour, it's never long before the next performance.

After welcoming the son of God into the world, you'll be set free to explore the rest of the park. A good first stop would be Creation—a laser show, religious lesson, and zoo exhibit rolled into one. In the beginning there is darkness, but it's soon broken by a green light that bursts through a pinhole, dancing and shimmering as a deep, Godly voice booms in Spanish. Thunder crashes, dry land is formed, and before you know what day it is, the world's first animals appear, rolling in on jerky wooden platforms with a sense of gravitas reminiscent of a high school play. A giraffe, an elephant, an animatronic gorilla. The show ends with the creation of Adam and Eve.

The park's food stands offer biblical favorites like empanadas and chicken shawarma, but if you're hoping for a last supper, you'll have

The Resurrection

to settle for a plastic reenactment—it's one of the park's thirty-seven exhibits dedicated to important events in the Bible. (Some of the titles— Veronica Washes Jesus's Face, Jesus Falls for a Third Time— make you wonder if they shouldn't have quit while they were ahead.) The park also includes a small temple, mosque, and, for reasons that are not entirely clear, an exhibit about Mahatma Gandhi.

But Tierra Santa's pièce de résistance is, of course, the resurrection—an attraction that, depending on your religious beliefs, can be breathtaking, sacrilegious, or just plain weird. Once every hour, park employees begin staring and pointing at the top of Crucifixion Mountain. As a crowd of onlookers focuses their cameras, a fifty-nine-foot-tall plastic Jesus rises up toward heaven, arms outstretched in a T. Slowly rotating, he blinks and turns his palms skyward as speakers hidden in fake palm trees blast the "Hallelujah" chorus, its triumphant melody broken only by the roar of passing planes.

52 | A VOMITORIUM

Here's a bit of cocktail trivia for you: a vomitorium is not actually a room where ancient Romans went to barf.

I know. You don't want to believe me—thanks to a misunderstanding popularized in many sixth-grade history classes, most people assume that a vomitorium is a room where Romans threw up after particularly heavy meals. This would seem to be a natural extension of other weird things the Romans did, like wear togas and speak Latin. But it's less strange to use an inflected language than it is to build a vomit room in your house. The Romans were no strangers to gluttony, but they didn't designate specific chambers to capture the results.

Instead, a vomitorium is an architectural term for a passageway in a theater that opens into a tier of seats. Think of the entrances in a typical sports stadium—you know, the tunnels that pop you out into the stands? Those are vomitoria. The name does share its root with *vomit*—both words come from the Latin verb *vomere* (to throw up, spew). And, depending on the event, they may very well contain nauseated fans. But the name *vomitorium* itself refers to the passages' ability to quickly move spectators into the stadium. Or, more graphically, to puke them out when the show is over.

53 MEDINAT AL-FAYOUM, EGYPT, ACCOMPANIED BY YOUR OWN SECURITY DETAIL

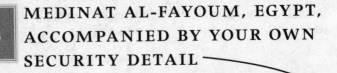

About eighty miles southwest of Cairo, Medinat al-Fayoum was once a holiday destination for thirteenth-century pharaohs; today's highlights include lesser-known pyramids and water wheels built by ancient Greek settlers. Since Medinat al-Fayoum attracts far fewer visitors than Cairo, it offers a welcome relief from busloads of camera-toting tourists at some of Egypt's major attractions.

However, it's also an easy place to get paranoid. After a horrific incident in 1997 where terrorists slaughtered sixty-three tourists at an archaeological site in Luxor, a city farther south, the leaders of Medinat al-Fayoum committed themselves to making sure nothing like that ever happened in their town. So whenever Western visitors come to the city, they're assigned their own security detail.

The problem is that no one tells you this. One traveler reported that after receiving a series of unexplained phone calls in his hotel room asking for the details of his itinerary, he and his girlfriend were stopped by a policeman on the street after dinner and told it was time to go to sleep. Once back at the hotel, they received another anonymous phone call instructing them where and when to have breakfast, and telling them that as soon as they visited the site, they'd be leaving town. Confused and scared, they spent the morning before their departure touring historical ruins with several men carrying assault rifles.

Once you realize that you're not being abducted, having a police escort can be a fun novelty—parading down the streets with your own bodyguards is a great way to pretend that you're important. But after a while, the Big Brother routine can get tiring, especially because most guards seem not to like their jobs. Instead of introducing themselves or acting as guides, they lurk in the background just close enough for you to know they're there. This is particularly awkward at mealtimes, when you and your traveling companion try to enjoy your food with a guard glaring at you from the next table.

If you're feeling naughty, you can try to evade your security detail—when's the last time these guys played a good game of cat and mouse? But considering that they're armed and cranky, it's probably best to just do what they say.

54 THE STEAM ROOM AT THE RUSSIAN & TURKISH BATHS

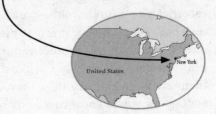

United States

New York

The Russian & Turkish Baths have been open in New York's East Village since 1892, and they're the real deal: a sauna, an ice-cold pool, Russian and Turkish steam rooms, and a cafeteria serving borscht and Polish sausage. After locking up your belongings and trading your clothing for a threadbare towel and sandals, you'll be set free to pick your preferred location to *schvitz* it out with a random assortment of old Russians, young hipsters, and everyone in between. If you've ever wondered what could be less pleasant than being smushed together with strangers in a crowded subway car in July, consider this: the baths are hotter, wetter, and on single-sex days, no one's wearing clothes.

The most interesting room in the baths is the Russian sauna, one of the only ones in the United States. For people with heart problems, it's also the most dangerous. Literally an oven, it's filled with twenty thousand pounds of rock that are heated overnight and left to cool during the day. They retain enough heat to keep the room nearly unbearable for hours after the oven is turned off. That explains the white plastic buckets and the spigots of ice-cold water—the custom is to sit in the room until the heat becomes excruciating, fill up an entire bucket of ice water, and then dump it over your head. Fans of the baths call the resulting experience a moment of "sheer delight," but a more accurate description would also include shock and a brief inability to breathe. If you are at risk for any sort of cardiac attack, this might not be your best choice.

If you want to really push your luck, sign up for a Platza Oak Leaf treatment, a traditional Russian treatment in which a spa attendant will lay you down, take a bundle of oak leaves soaked in olive oil soap, and beat you. (The leaves, which are naturally astringent, exfoliate the skin and open the pores.) More often than not, this treatment will occur in the Russian sauna itself, which means that not only will it be observed by everyone in the room, but that, oppressed by the heat, you might suffocate. Then, just before you pass out, your body will be subjected to its final shock: the attendant will have you sit up, close your eyes, and, without warning, slowly pour two buckets of ice water over your head.

55 THE BLARNEY STONE

Ireland

No one is really sure where the Blarney Stone came from. Some say it could have been part of Jerusalem's Wailing Wall, brought to Ireland during the Crusades. Others claim it's a piece of the Stone of Scone given to Cormac MacCarthy in 1314 to thank him for his help in the Battle of Bannockburn. Some even think it's the rock that Moses struck with his staff to provide water to the Israelites. "Whatever the truth of its origin, we believe a witch saved from drowning revealed its power to the MacCarthys," the Blarney Castle Web site announces, simultaneously dodging the question and discrediting itself as a reliable source of information.

Regardless of which, if any, of these rumors are true, there's still no explanation for why a stone of such importance would have been inconspicuously incorporated into the exterior wall of a fifteenth-century castle. But that's not the point. Set into the battlements of Blarney Castle, about five miles from the Irish town of Cork, the block of bluestone is said to bestow anyone who kisses it with great eloquence and talent in empty flattery. So for over two hundred years, pilgrims from around the world have been planting wet ones on the stone's surface in hopes that they too will be blessed with the so-called "gift of gab."

Unfortunately for would-be orators, the stone does not lend itself naturally to public displays of affection. Reaching it requires climbing to the top of the castle, leaning backward over a parapet, and dangling much of your body in the air, angling for a kiss as you gaze at the ground looming several stories below. In the good old days before liability waivers, visitors were held by the ankles and lowered headfirst over the wall. Now there are metal rails to help support and guide you, and a protective grate that prevents uncoordinated tourists from falling to their deaths.

The stone's actual powers are debatable, but one thing's for sure—the Blarney Stone is a germaphobe's nightmare. Kissed by more than four hundred thousand people per year, it's covered with trace bits of spit left behind with every pucker. Smooching it might not give you the gift of gab, but you could take home a different souvenir: a saliva-transmitted affliction like herpes, warts, or glandular fever. At least you're safe from meningitis—to get it from kissing, you'd have to use a lot of tongue.

XXXX MICHAEL BALDWIN XXXX

Mexico City on the First Day of the Swine Flu Outbreak

My timing in visiting other countries hasn't always been the greatest. My first trip to Beijing happened just after America had bombed the Chinese embassy in Yugoslavia. (Nothing says "Welcome" like a mob stoning your embassy.) Two years later, I bought a return flight from Paris to New York for September 13, 2001. Two years after that, I went to Rio de Janeiro, only to be greeted by drug gangs setting fire to city buses. So when I arrived in Mexico City for a weeklong vacation on the exact day that swine flu hit, it was par for the course.

I boarded my overnight flight in ignorant bliss and, since news of the outbreak didn't come out until a couple of hours after we took off, I arrived at the Mexico City airport in ignorant bliss as well. Determined to experience the "real" Mexico as soon as possible, I decided to take the metro instead of a taxi.

That's when I had the first sense that something was wrong: standing on the platform, I noticed several people wearing blue surgical-type face masks. Funny, I thought. Mexico City may not be known for the cleanest air, but this seemed a bit extreme.

I spent the morning walking around the historical center, becoming increasingly puzzled by the masks. But I still didn't think much of them until I stopped by my hotel to ask the man at reception where I could find out about concerts going on that night.

"There aren't any," he said.

That didn't make any sense. This was Friday night in a major world city. The problem must have been my Spanish, so I tried simpler words.

"Music. Tonight. Where?" I played some air guitar to reinforce the message.

"Everything's closed," he replied.

Confused, I found another tourist in the lobby and asked him what was going on. "There's this pig flu going around," he said. "The government's closed all public spaces." I checked an Internet terminal, and sure enough, the very first news headline for the entire world was: "Swine Flu Shuts Down Mexico City." I had apparently spent a half month's salary on a plane ticket to Ground Zero of a deadly plague.

Convinced of my imminent death, I tried to find distractions. But the government's shutdown of all public venues—concerts, restaurants, nightclubs, even archaeological sites—left me with nothing to do. Instead I took to wandering the near-empty streets and amusing myself by keeping track of people with unusual face masks, like a woman who'd decorated hers with a smiley face, or a goth kid with a spiked collar and spiked hair whose all-black color scheme was rudely disrupted by his mask's bright blue.

It was a lonely experience, which was made worse by the fact that Mexico City is at a ridiculously high elevation, so the air is extremely dry. Which, not being used to it, made me cough. A lot. Which, naturally, made everyone around me assume I had swine flu. And would kill them.

Then, on Monday, a 5.6 earthquake hit Mexico City.

Still, it wasn't all bad. On Tuesday night, a Mexican friend of mine was determined to take me out *somewhere*. After calling his friends all over the city, he found the only thing open—an

Irish pub that was technically outside the city limits, and thus not subject to the closing restrictions. So, in a metropolitan area of almost nine million people, we went to the trendiest, most happening nightspot there was. Five other patrons were there. At least they had tequila.

MICHAEL BALDWIN is the creator of the CommonCensus Map Project.

✕✕✕✕

56 THE WIENER'S CIRCLE

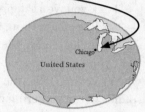

Chicago
United States

In terms of food, the Wiener's Circle, a hot dog joint in Chicago's Lincoln Park, doesn't stand out much from its competition. It's got greasy burgers; it's got cheese fries. What makes it different is its attitude: show up late on a Saturday night, and your food is likely to come with a side of screaming douchebags.

That's because the Wiener's Circle staff has made a game of insulting its customers, serving up orders with catch phrases like "For here or to go, motherfucker?" and "Pay me my money or get the fuck out." According to the Wiener's Circle's owners, Barry Nemerow and Larry Gold, this tradition started accidentally when Larry, frustrated that he couldn't get his patron's attention, called a customer an asshole. That was fifteen years ago; these days they estimate that the Wiener's Circle's free-for-all nastiness has doubled their business.

If they were all playful, the back-and-forth insults might be okay. But as the night wears on and the patrons get drunker, a side of humanity begins to show that, as a video segment on *This American Life* pointed out, is better left unseen. The Wiener's Circle is a microcosm of segregation in Chicago, with a black staff catering to a predominantly white clientele. Add alcohol, a hot kitchen, and an atmosphere free from the usual rules of social interaction, and the results aren't pretty.

"Nice headband, you fuckin' whore," said one customer caught on camera.

"Fuck you, you sagging slut," said another.

"It's like an abortion, bitch!" shouted a different patron, presumably about his cheese fries. "I'm eating your babies and you love it!"

If you order a hot dog during the day, you should be fine. But when evening falls, the Wiener's Circle becomes exactly what it sounds like: a gathering place for dicks.

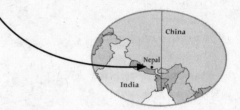

R eally? You really want to see the top of Mount Everest before you die? Why—because you want to boast to your friends that you've climbed the world's tallest mountain?* Or is it because you want the thrill of adventure that comes from paying $65,000 for a guided climb and then risking a team of sherpas' lives (not to mention your own) so that you can spend fifteen minutes breathing supplemental oxygen at the so-called top of the world? Unless you love frostbite, hypoxia, blinding snow, and high-altitude games of Russian roulette, do Nepal a favor and stay home.

---

* It's actually not. Measured from base to summit, Mauna Kea in Hawaii is taller, if mostly underwater.

58 GARBAGE CITY

Cairo
Egypt

Garbage City is a reeking slum on the outskirts of Cairo that's covered, literally, in trash. There's trash in the streets; there's trash in the houses. People live in it, work in it, and sometimes even sleep in it. And every day, there's more. In fact, residents go out of their way to bring it home. Carried in by donkey in huge sacks, the trash, ironically, is what helps the neighborhood survive.

The slum's residents are the Zabbaleen, the garbage people. Together with their pigs, which until recently ran freely through the streets gorging themselves on trash, the Zabbaleen used to take away about half of the sixty-five hundred tons of refuse the city produces each day. After separating valuable garbage like plastic, metal, and glass, the Zabbaleen fed anything organic to their pigs, which were not just garbage disposals, but an important source of meat—the Zabbaleen are Coptic Christians, and unlike the Muslim majority, they eat pork.

I say "used to" because in the spring of 2009, the government ordered the killing of all of Cairo's pigs. Supposedly this was to prevent swine flu (a strange claim, given that no pig has been shown to carry it), but the Zabbaleen think it was a political move.

Regardless of the reason, the results have been disastrous. The Zabbaleen, down a major source of food, have stopped taking away most of Cairo's waste. With no effective way to replace them, streets are piled with stinking heaps of trash, and the government is struggling to compensate for a system that it itself destroyed. In the meantime, the term "garbage city" applies to all of Cairo.

Built in several stages between 3000 and 1600 B.C., Stonehenge is one of the mysteries of the ancient world. Was it a temple? An astrological observatory? A burial site? No one's really sure.

What we do know: its stones each weigh more than fifty tons, and some of them came from as far as 240 miles away. All this was accomplished in days when a shovel made from a cow's shoulder blade was cutting-edge technology. So whatever Stonehenge was for must have been pretty damn important.

Unfortunately, Stonehenge no longer commands the same level of respect. Tucked into what is now the Wiltshire countryside, it's cut off from its surrounding fields by a chain-link fence. A large parking lot sits nearby with a gift shop, ice-cream vendors, Port-O-Potties, and a subterranean visitors' center. Worst, the A344 highway passes so close that some people save money on the admission price by just looking at it from the road.

Consider following their lead. Thanks to previous problems with vandalism, visitors are no longer permitted to actually approach the stones. Instead an entrance fee of more than $10 only allows you to walk around the periphery of the circle, kept at a safe distance by a wire guardrail. (The main benefit of this experience, as compared to viewing it from the road, is that it allows you to take photographs of Stonehenge with the highway in the background.) Up close, you'll find that the stones are not nearly as large as postcards make them seem, and whatever spiritual experience you may have hoped for is likely to be destroyed by busloads of tourists walking in dazed circles as they listen to the audio tour.

If you insist on visiting, pay the extra money and sign up for a before- or after-hours private access tour, which will let you get as close to the stones as you want. Or, alternatively, plan a visit in June—perhaps in keeping with its original purpose, Stonehenge hosts a great party for the summer solstice.

60 THE KHEWRA SALT MINES MOSQUE

S peaking of Stonehenge, does anyone remember the scene in *This Is Spinal Tap* where the band commissions a full-size model of Stonehenge for the set of an upcoming show, but, thanks to a mislabeled diagram, ends up with one that's eighteen inches high? (It's lowered onto the stage and then attacked by dancing elves. Anyone?)

That's what the mosque at Pakistan's Khewra Salt Mines reminds me of.

This is not a criticism of salt mine tourism. You should, for example, visit the Wieliczka Salt Mine in Poland. Over a thousand feet deep, Wieliczka was on the original list of UNESCO World Heritage Sites for the incredible salt statues created by some of its workers. Modern sculptors continued the tradition and the mine is now home to salt replicas of everything from Da Vinci's *The Last Supper* to Pope John Paul II. Best is the salt cathedral—a cavernous room lined with friezes whose floors, ceilings, altars, and even chandeliers are all made from salt.

So at first I was excited to hear that there was a Pakistani salt mosque—score one for religious equality! But the real salt mosque is disappointingly small. How small? You can sit on it. Instead of being a soaring saline tribute to one of the world's largest religions, it's closer in scale to a gingerbread house.

Of course, since the mine extends about a dozen stories underground, there's more to see at Khewra than just the salt mosque—for example, an assembly hall with backlit walls and a replica of the Great Wall of China. But be prepared: it too is smaller than the real thing.

61 ANYWHERE ON A YAMAHA RHINO

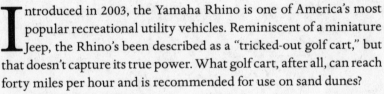

Introduced in 2003, the Yamaha Rhino is one of America's most popular recreational utility vehicles. Reminiscent of a miniature Jeep, the Rhino's been described as a "tricked-out golf cart," but that doesn't capture its true power. What golf cart, after all, can reach forty miles per hour and is recommended for use on sand dunes?

And that's not all it does.

To quote from the legal complaint for an anti-Rhino class action lawsuit:

> The Yamaha Rhino is prone to tip over and seriously injure its occupants due to several defects, including its top-heavy design, dangerously narrow track width, high center of gravity, wheels that are too small to maintain stability, steering geometry that facilitates rollovers and tip overs even at low speeds and on flat terrain, heavy rigid steel roll cage that has no safety padding, lack of doors, leg guards, or other enclosures to protect occupants, lack of handholds or handles for passengers, and defective restraint systems.

Perhaps unsurprisingly, Rhinos have been involved in a lot of accidents, causing everything from head, back, and neck wounds to severe crush injuries that often require surgery or amputation. According to the U.S. Consumer Safety Commission, at least forty-six drivers or passengers have been killed by Rhinos, including several cases where people were thrown from their RUV and then smushed when the half-ton vehicle landed on them.

In 2009, thanks to pressure from lawsuits and the U.S. Consumer Safety Commission, Yamaha announced a free repair program that retrofits Rhinos with several safety features that lessen the likelihood of a rollover and help prevent people from flying out. For example, doors. But they still haven't recalled the Rhino—instead they continue to market it as a family-friendly off-road vehicle.

Ride at your own risk.

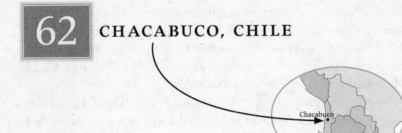

62 | CHACABUCO, CHILE

Chacabuco

Chile

The tiny town of Chacabuco, Chile, has never been a tourist hotspot—it's in the middle of the Atacama Desert, one of the driest places on earth. Founded in 1924 by the Lautaro Nitrate Company Ltd., Chacabuco started off as a mining town for sodium nitrate, an ingredient in fertilizer that used to be one of Chile's major exports. But sodium nitrate is also an important ingredient for bombs, and during World War I, Germany perfected a method of creating it synthetically on a large scale. That was great news for Germany, but it devastated Chile's economy. Chacabuco closed down in 1938, making it one of 170 nitrate ghost towns scattered through the Atacama.

Being a ghost town would have been bad enough. But then in 1973, Pinochet decided to turn it into a concentration camp. For the next year and a half it held between six hundred and one thousand political prisoners, who lived in former mining quarters that had been turned into barracks.

For a prison, Chacabuco's location is ideal. Stretching some six hundred miles up and down the Chilean coast, the Atacama Desert is fifty times drier than Death Valley and is lifeless except for some algae, lichen, and the occasional cactus. The landscape is so desolate that NASA has used it as a practice ground for life-detecting robots, and in *Space Odyssey: Voyage to the Planets*, the Atacama played the role of Mars. Any escapees would have quickly died of dehydration and been turned into mummies, which makes the fact that the Chilean army surrounded Chacabuco with nearly one hundred land mines seem like a bit of overkill.

If you decide to visit, you'll get a warm welcome from the town's sole resident, Pedro Barreda, who has devoted the past few years of his life to protecting and preserving the town. With a daily schedule that consists mostly of tending to a few plants and tidying up his living quarters, Barreda loves showing people around. He doesn't charge anything for the tours, but if you feel like bringing a thank-you gift, he'd certainly appreciate some water.

China

Dongguan

ocated in the muggy, smoggy city of Dongguan, the South China Mall opened in 2005 to much excitement: with 7.1 million square feet of retail space, it's one of the largest shopping centers in the world. Replete with an amusement park, IMAX theater, and hotel complex—not to mention a full-size Arc de Triomphe—it was built in anticipation of seventy thousand visitors a day.

Alas, those shoppers never came. As of June 2008, there were fewer than a dozen stores operating in a shopping complex built to accommodate fifteen hundred. Instead of bustling with shoppers, its long hallways were quiet, abandoned except for a few bored sales-clerks and the occasional security guard. Escalators stood still, their railings covered in dust-coated plastic. From the very beginning, business was so bad that some of its monuments weren't even finished. "The mall entered the world pre-ruined," wrote one reporter, "as if its developers had deliberately created an attraction for people with a taste for abandonment and decay."

But if the mall itself is depressing, its marketing material is aggressively cheery. "Do you want to take a dreamlike journey?" it asks in a description of the Amazing World, an indoor/outdoor amusement center—and one of the mall's only functional features—that is supposedly "full of excitement, scream, fashion and joy." There is a roller coaster. There is a log flume ride (though it sometimes lacks water). There is a free fall ride that asks visitors whether they would like to "experience the feeling of 'death.'" As if that's not enough, "there are other peculiar amusement activities suitable for the old and the young." "Bumping car, Wizard of Oz, Self-enjoyment"— there's even a "special area for naughty children."

If only some would visit.

An empty store in the South China Mall

LISA MARGONELLI ✕✕✕✕

Sumqayit, Azerbaijan

Oh! Sumqayit, Azerbaijan! Once, you made all the petro-chemicals the Soviet Union could consume. Once, your massive factories, your lurching cooling towers, your python-esque pipes must have gleamed in the wintry sun of the Caspian! Your workers walked in throngs, carrying the extra rations of milk and cheese they received to prevent bone loss. But all that ended, and now you are rusting. Workless, people dig holes in the ground, hoping to sell the dirt. What remains is the pollution, enough to put little Sumqayit on both *Time* magazine's and *Scientific American's* lists of the top ten most polluted places on earth in 2007. Given that, the absolute sad-dest place on earth can be found in the city cemetery, which is crowded with tiny graves that are the result of Sumqayit's hor-rendously high infant mortality rate. Azeri graves often have photographs of the deceased, and here they are of well-dressed children with birth defects, obviously much loved during their short lives. There are restaurants in Sumqayit, but the longer I stayed in town, the more terrifying the idea of consuming local food became—so I recommend bringing snacks and water with you from Baku, thirty kilometers away.

LISA MARGONELLI is the author of *Oil on the Brain: Petroleum's Long, Strange Trip to Your Tank.*

✕✕✕✕

AN ISLAND OFF GERMANY'S EAST COAST, JANUARY 16, 1362

Imagine the scene: you're a German farmer in the mid-1300s, diligently tending your livestock in your field on the island of Strand. In the distance you can see the buildings of Rungholt, Strand's main port, and beyond that the North Sea. You're working hard but you're happy—your wife's pregnant again, and your youngest sons are just old enough to start helping out on the farm. You take a moment's break to gaze out into the distance, giving thanks for all that is good, and that's when you realize that something is not right. The clouds are dark and rushing toward you. The wind is screaming. Your rudimentary hoe is blown out of your hands just as the sky erupts into pelting, horizontal rain. You try to run to shelter, but you never make it. The storm is too strong. The sea rises up and enormous waves crash over the island. You, your family, and your entire community are killed.

No, it's not the apocalypse. It's the Grote Mandrenke, Low Saxon for "the Great Man-Drowning"—a massive cyclonic windstorm that hit the northern European coast on January 16, 1362. The *mandrenke* was so *grote* that it killed at least twenty-five thousand people, de-stroyed some sixty Danish parishes, sank the entire city of Rung-holt, and smashed the German coast into islands. Not bad for a day's work—and not a good day to have been there.

65 FUCKING, AUSTRIA

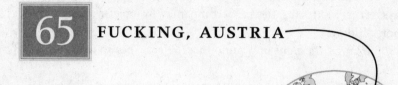

In 2004, the residents of the small Austrian town of Fucking took a vote on whether to change their village's name. Our town can't be mentioned on international television, argued the proponents of a switch. And besides, it wouldn't be the first time a group of people abandoned what they considered an embarrassing moniker: the Canadian village of Gayside is now known as Baytona.

But the good people of Fucking decided that no, they did not want to change the name. They were proud of their home, this hamlet of just over one hundred people, founded in 1070 and named after a man named Focko. Besides, a good part of their annual GDP came from T-shirt sales.

There was one problem, however: the town's road signs. Long considered tempting trophies by immature tourists, they have been stolen more times than the town's budget could afford. So Fucking's leaders came up with a plan. They commissioned new signs, bolted to steel posts that were embedded in a concrete block—a creation so sturdy that according to Fucking's mayor, it would take all night to steal. And in an attempt to kill two birds with one stone, they decided to address another local nuisance at the same time: speeding. So right below the town name they hung a different placard that says, BITTE, NICHT SO SCHNELL, accompanied by a picture of two cartoon children.

"Fucking," the signs now announce. "Please, not so fast."

Skip Fucking, but you might want to check out the Newfoundland town of Dildo. It's home to the Dildo Museum interpretive center and everyone's favorite summer event, the Historic Dildo Days.

One of Fucking's former stealable signs

66 THE WHITE SHARK CAFÉ WHILE DRESSED AS AN ELEPHANT SEAL

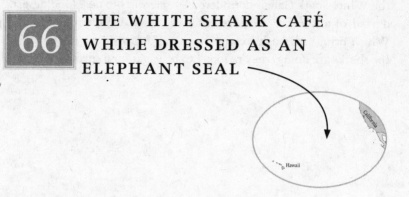

I know you think it's an unlikely situation: you, floating in the middle of the Pacific Ocean, dressed as an elephant seal. But it's not like it's impossible. You're at a costume party on a cruise boat from Hawaii, there's free booze, you decide to reenact the "I'm the king of the world!" scene from *Titanic*, and then, boom. You fall overboard.

Please make sure this doesn't happen. If there's one spot you don't want to go swimming in a seal outfit, it's the four-hundred-mile-wide stretch of ocean halfway between Hawaii and Baja, California. Known to scientists as the "White Shark Café," this is a popular congregation spot for great whites, who come to the café from all along the North American coast to spend some quality time—sometimes months—hanging out with other sharks. They swim in circles; they participate in mysterious dives. Eventually, they return to the coast for their favorite time of year: elephant seal breeding season.

No one's really sure what attracts the sharks to the café or, for that matter, what they eat while they're there—despite its name, the White Shark Café is considered by scientists to be a food desert, devoid of any other creatures that the great whites might enjoy. Which brings me back to why you shouldn't visit: no matter what the sharks are doing, they're likely to be eager for a snack.

67 THE SIDEWALK OUTSIDE THE ROMAN COLISEUM DURING THE CRAZY GLADIATOR'S SHIFT

I f you visit Rome you should, of course, go to the Coliseum. But do not linger on the sidewalk outside.

I say this because of the gladiators. No, not the ghosts of the thousands of men slaughtered in the Coliseum's ring to give nobles something to do on a Sunday afternoon. I'm talking about the modern-day gladiators: the guys in sandals and capes who accost tourists outside the coliseum's entrance, offering to pose for photographs in exchange for tips.

Most of these gladiators are harmless, more interested in carrying on loud cell phone conversations with their girlfriends than they are in accurately portraying ancient Rome. But there is one gladiator who takes his role-playing more seriously than the rest. Trust me: you'll know him when you see him.

I caught my first glimpse of his feathered helmet and silver face mask as I took a gelato break on a nearby stone bench, and it didn't take me long to realize that this gladiator was different. The other gladiators smiled and posed for photographs with people who had voluntarily approached them. The crazy gladiator grabbed a woman off the street, hoisted her above his head with a grunt, and held her hostage until her boyfriend had taken a picture. The other gladiators let kids touch their swords. The crazy gladiator seized a small girl by the back of her overalls and pretended to plunge his trident into her stomach as her flustered parents struggled to find their wallets. The other gladiators attracted children by letting them try on their helmets. The crazy gladiator had a net.

The tactic worked. He drew a crowd. And I, a person who experiences a rush of anxiety any time I see a mime, decided that I wanted a picture with him.

I handed the camera to my friend Mark, and we approached, feigning calm. This did not fool the crazy gladiator. "Ah! Christians to kill!" he shouted in English. He ran at us, trident raised, and grabbed me by the neck. "Come over here!" he said, gesturing toward a fellow gladiator. "Christians to kill! I *love* killing Christians!" His friend obliged, holding a plastic sword to my throat as the crazy gladiator pointed his trident toward my chest and yelled, "Silicone, ha ha ha!" as Mark snapped a photo.

I barely had a chance to recover from this public reference to my (decidedly silicone-free) chest before the crazy gladiator grabbed our camera, handed it to his friend, and pulled us both toward him for another shot. Then he angled the trident toward Mark's crotch and gave the camera a worried look and a thumbs-down.

Luckily, no breasts or testicles were actually harmed in the making of our photographs. Instead, the second gladiator snapped a final picture, turned to Mark, and said, "You tip the gladiators, yes?" And like countless tourists before us, we nodded and pulled out our wallets, grateful to have escaped.

68 ANY PLACE WHOSE PRIMARY CLAIM TO FAME IS A LARGE FIBERGLASS THING

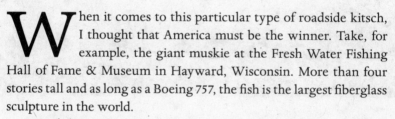

When it comes to this particular type of roadside kitsch, I thought that America must be the winner. Take, for example, the giant muskie at the Fresh Water Fishing Hall of Fame & Museum in Hayward, Wisconsin. More than four stories tall and as long as a Boeing 757, the fish is the largest fiberglass sculpture in the world.

But while we might have the biggest, Australia has the most: it's home to more than 150 giant roadside sculptures, which are affectionately known as Big Things and are becoming recognized as a type of folk art.

It all started with the Big Banana. Built in 1964 at Coffs Harbour, it's since been joined by scores of oversize creations, from the twelve-ton Giant Koala to the Big Merino, an enormous sheep known to fans as Rambo. There's the Big Golden Gumboot, the Big Trout, and the Big Cigar. Sometimes the sculptures are cartoonish (the Big Boxing Crocodile); sometimes they're mundane (the Big Coffee Pot). They can even be scatological—the Big Poo appeared briefly in 2002 as a protest against sewage ocean dumping. But more commonly they celebrate food, as is the case with the Big Oyster, Big Cherries, the Big Mango, and the Big Lobster (known to locals as Larry). Some represent things you don't really *want* to see larger-than-life: witness Big Mosquito.

Clustered mostly in the southeast, Australia's Big Things have a campy appeal that makes it fun to take a picture next to one or two. But before you join the trend of people scheduling road trips to see all 150, be sure to evaluate your priorities: to visit *every* Big Thing, you'd have to drive the circumference of Australia.

69 THE PATH OF AN ADVANCING COLUMN OF DRIVER ANTS

If you don't relish the idea of spending your vacation being attacked by flesh-eating insects, you should stay clear of driver ants. Native to the African rain forest, they protect themselves by plunging their giant, razor-sharp jaws into anything that stands in their way. Get pinched by one driver ant and you'll have two irritating puncture wounds; get pinched by a colony and your African safari will come to a quick and gruesome end.

Luckily, driver ants travel in groups of up to twenty million, which makes them pretty easy to avoid. "Viewed from afar, a huge raiding column of a driver ant colony seems like a single living entity, a giant amoeba spreading across 70 meters of ground," says Bert Hölldobler, an expert on the species. The ants also prefer the taste of insects to human flesh and, thanks to their tendency to eat anything in front of them, are excellent for pest control—provided that you're not home at the time of their visit. If you are home and are for some reason immobilized, however, you could be eaten alive.

In the unlikely case that that happens, here are some interesting facts to distract you from the searing pain: driver ants are blind, so they communicate through pheromones. Fertile males are driven out of the colony when they're young and spend their pubescent weeks developing into gross-looking winged insects whose bloated abdomens give them their even grosser nickname: "sausage flies." Once a sausage fly reaches sexual maturity, he sniffs out a nearby driver ant column and then plops himself down in its path. The other ants swarm on top of him and, as if punishing a philandering husband, rip off his wings. Once he's been suitably incapacitated, the ants carry the sausage fly off to a virgin queen, who nabs a lifetime's worth of sperm, and then leaves him to die.

I would also not recommend seeing a column of driver ants from the perspective of a sausage fly.

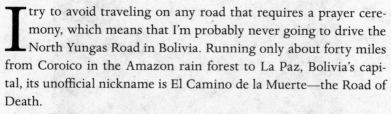

I try to avoid traveling on any road that requires a prayer ceremony, which means that I'm probably never going to drive the
North Yungas Road in Bolivia. Running only about forty miles
from Coroico in the Amazon rain forest to La Paz, Bolivia's capital, its unofficial nickname is El Camino de la Muerte—the Road of
Death.

Its official nickname is no more reassuring: in 1995, the Inter-
American Development Bank declared Yungas the World's Most
Dangerous Road. It's been known to kill between two hundred and
three hundred people a year; during one particularly bad stretch,
twenty-five vehicles went over the edge in one twelve-month period—
an average of about one every two weeks. The road is so dreaded
that locals stop to present an offering to the goddess Pachamama—
Bolivian for "Mother Earth"—before they drive it. Pachamama apparently enjoys beer; unfortunately, so do many Yungas drivers.

Look at a photograph of the road and it's obvious why death is
a concern. Despite being used for two-way traffic, there are spots
where it is no more than ten feet across. The road is carved into a

mountainside, which means that on one side is a rock wall; on the other is a drop of anywhere from twenty to three thousand feet. It is unpaved. There are no guardrails. In rainy season, it turns to mud; landslides frequently wipe out entire sections. It also used to be the main route between La Paz and Coroico, which means it was crowded with buses and trucks driven by men chewing coca leaves to calm their nerves. Unsurprisingly, the road is dotted with crosses and memorials to people who have lost their lives.

In an effort to improve safety, Yungas has its own rules. Descending traffic always yields to ascending. When passing, cars drive on the left side of the road instead of Bolivia's usual right—that way, the driver on the outside will be better able to tell if his wheels are about

Here's hoping that there's not a truck around the corner.

to go over the edge. For a brief period, the road was closed to two-way traffic—a life-saving move that was reversed when truck drivers complained that they were losing too much revenue.

The biggest improvement came in 2006, when a long-awaited new road—paved and far less precipitous—opened after twenty years of construction. Most people choose it instead, but that doesn't mean Yungas Road is empty. Truck drivers still occasionally use it, and it's begun to attract a new group of thrill-seekers: mountain bikers. With a near-continuous descent that takes between five and six hours to ride, it's got breathtaking (and occasionally life-taking) views—and now that there's less traffic, it's safer than it's ever been. Though then again, that's not really saying much.

×××× **ERIC SIMONS** ××××

Adventure of the Beagle, the Musical

There's a ton of stuff worth doing in Tierra del Fuego, should you find yourself there. Beautiful glaciers, for one. Also: rugged history, scenic sheep, and epic trout.

On the other side of things, there's the *Adventure of the Beagle*, the musical. You might not be able to die a happy person without having seen Tierra del Fuego's wildlife, but I promise, you'll do just fine without *La Aventura del Beagle*.

Based loosely—by which I mean, essentially, not really at all—on the 1830s voyage of the young Charles Darwin and his mates through South America, *el espactaculo del fin del mundo*— the "show at the end of the earth"—is the sort of production aimed primarily at cruise ship passengers. (Better options: Go to the onboard karaoke night! Dress up in a tux and try to learn Dutch from the captain! Jump overboard and try to swim to Antarctica!)

The *Beagle* musical takes one of the highlights of the voyage, the amazing scenery, and renders it in jagged bedsheet glaciers. It features a swarm of indigenous people played by grunting Muppets on sticks, and a group of sailors dressed in what can only be described as Parisian pastry-chef hats.

Yes, all this is bad. But what truly elevates the *Adventure of the Beagle*, the musical, into lunacy, is the singing, dancing, twenty-foot-tall fossilized giant sloth-like thing. The sloth-like thing chides Darwin in a wonderful basso profundo. It cavorts around the stage on puppet strings and appears to be made in part of NERF. It is also fluorescent green.

Naturally, the fluorescent green fossilized giant sloth-like thing is given a starring role.

We should back up a bit.

In real life, the twenty-three-year-old Charles Darwin arrived in middle Patagonia, somewhere near modern-day Bahia Blanca, in 1832. Bored out of his mind with watching the coastal sand hillocks go by ("I never knew before, what a horrid ugly object a sand hillock is," he wrote in a letter home), and seasick from tossing about in a small boat in the fierce Patagonian wind, Darwin rejoiced at the chance to go ashore to do some fossil-hunting. One of the fossils they turned up was a giant sloth jawbone, and Darwin went on over the next few years to find several more fossilized *Megatherium* bits scattered around the Patagonian plains. If he was not the first to discover it, the fossils he sent home were at least useful in advancing *Megatherium* science, and hey, everyone loves a good giant sloth tale. Oh, and fossils—those have to do with Darwin, right?

So in the musical, the extinct sloth appears at the crucial apex of the drama, the beginning of the second act, just after the section titled "FitzRoy's Rage" in which the narrow-minded captain bellows at Darwin for believing in fossils. (In real life, FitzRoy wrote in his own journal about his "friend" discovering the "interesting and valuable remains of extinct animals.")

The sloth, though, makes it clear it isn't standing for any creationist captains on *this* voyage.

"You can try to deny what your eyes meet / With some pastimes or a trip off to sea," the sloth sings. "Go hunting, or some bingo, chess, perhaps football / Or maybe a sudden step out to the music hall. / But the more you try and try / You'll just have to change your mind / 'Cause after all you really know / I am as real as these bones."

And then: dancing! The sloth jerks across the back of the

stage, in a kind of hip-bone-connected-to-the-leg-bone kind of way. Once finished, it toddles off and the play wears on.

Many of the great stories of history are just as great on the stage: *Les Misérables*, say, or *Monty Python's Spamalot*. But when it comes to Tierra del Fuego and *La Aventura del Beagle*, it's best to stick to the original source material. Or just go for the scenic sheep.

ERIC SIMONS is the author of *Darwin Slept Here: Discovery, Adventure, and Swimming Iguanas in Charles Darwin's South America.*

✕✕✕✕

CUSCO, IF YOU ARE ALBINO

Since Cusco is the capital city of the ancient Inca Empire and a jumping off point for Machu Picchu, you may well find yourself there before you die. But don't forget your sunblock. As befits the former home of a sun-worshipping civilization, it has the highest levels of UV radiation in the world.

To identify the world's worst spot, researchers examined UV data from NASA's Total Ozone Mapping Spectrometer between 1997 and 2003. They decided that despite the fact that Australia and New Zealand have the world's highest rates of skin cancer, the highest UV levels were in the Peruvian Andes. With a UV index score of 25, Cusco came in at the top of the list.

To give you a sense of how high 25 is, consider that much like the stereo in *This Is Spinal Tap*, the scale usually only goes up to 11. The Environmental Protection Agency issues UV Alerts for anything over 6. At 11 or higher, exposed skin can burn in minutes, and the EPA and World Health Organization recommend staying inside as much as possible, which is fine for normal workdays, but not a feasible option when hiking the Inca Trail.

72 MANNEKEN PIS

Considering its name, any tourists who make a special trip to Brussels to see Manneken Pis have only themselves to blame. Yes, it's weird that one of Brussels' most famous attractions is a bronze sculpture of a naked boy urinating into a basin. But its name means "little pee man." What exactly did you expect to see?

There's nothing diminutive, however, about the statue's popularity—it's spawned an entire industry of Manneken-themed T-shirts and coffee mugs (I have a pencil sharpener), and has become an unofficial emblem of the city. It even has a fan club, the Friends of Manneken Pis, and a wardrobe: FOMP members have created more than eight hundred costumes for the boy. Depending on what day you show up, he might be dressed as anyone from Napoléon to Nelson Mandela; on truly special days, the Friends of Manneken Pis make the statue pee beer.

Accounts of the sculpture's inspiration vary. Perhaps it is in honor of a two-year-old duke who, in 1142, was hung in a basket from a tree by his troops and then urinated on his army's opponents. Perhaps it is a tribute to Juliaanske, a small boy from Brussels who is said to have saved the city walls from dynamite by peeing on a burning fuse. Or perhaps it's simply in memory of a small boy gone missing, later found relieving himself in a garden. No one really knows.

Manneken Pis will likely fulfill most tourists' quota for urinating statues. But if you still want more, check out his sister—her name is Jeanneke Pis, and she lives just up the street. Created in the mid-1980s by Denis-Adrien Debouvrie, the pig-tailed Jeanneke is cuter than her brother but no less naughty. Naked and smiling, she squats on top of a limestone pedestal and gazes blissfully toward the sky, as water drips from between her legs in a realistic tinkle.

Manneken Pis

Jeanneke Pis

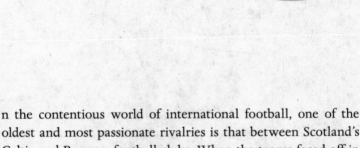

73 AN OLD FIRM DERBY WHILE WEARING THE WRONG COLOR T-SHIRT

In the contentious world of international football, one of the oldest and most passionate rivalries is that between Scotland's Celtic and Rangers football clubs. When the teams faced off in the first Old Firm derby—a game where the two teams go head-to-head—the press described the match as a "friendly encounter." That hospitality, however, didn't last long.

Part of the problem is the deep differences between Celtic and Rangers fans. Both teams are Scottish, but Celtic was founded in 1887 by a Catholic monk whose specific goal was to create a charity to help alleviate poverty in Glasgow's Irish community. Rangers were the preferred team of the relatively comfortable Scottish Protestant majority; they didn't even allow Catholics on the team till 1989. Adding to the conflict, Celtic fans tend to be Irish nationalists, whereas Rangers are unionists.

These differences can be explosive. On Old Firm weekends, admission rates for local hospitals increase ninefold, and the cumulative total for arrests at Old Firm derbies is the highest of any game in the world. After Celtic beat the Rangers 1–0 in the Scottish Cup Final at Hampden in 1980, more than nine thousand angry fans stormed the field in one of the largest on-field battles ever reported.

Which brings me to my point. Celtic's color is green. Rangers' is blue. If you don't feel passionately about either side, you'd be wise to pick an outfit in a more neutral hue.

74 THE ANNUAL POISON OAK SHOW

If evil were a plant, it would be poison oak. Prevalent up and down the United States' Pacific coast, poison oak produces an oil called urushiol that causes a dermatologic version of hell—a weeping, itchy rash that can last for more than a month. About 85 percent of people are susceptible to urushiol, and as little as a billionth of a gram can cause a reaction, which means that a quarter of an ounce, judiciously applied, could cause a rash on every person on earth.

Given urushiol's power, the idea of hosting a poison oak festival sounds stupid, if not sadistic. And yet every September for the past twenty-five years, the town of Columbia, California, has done exactly that. With categories based on a traditional flower show, it encourages people to bring in their finest specimens of poison oak to be judged in contests like Best Arrangement of Poison Oak, Best Poison Oak Accessory or Jewelry, and Most Potent Looking Red Leaves. There's even a competition for the Best Photo of Poison Oak Rash and—I shudder to even mention this—the Most Original Poison Oak Dish.

Before you rush to enter, keep in mind that urushiol, being oil, doesn't evaporate, so it can stay on your shoes or gloves or bouquet-making tools for years. If you accidentally burn the stuff, you can get a reaction in your lungs. Think you're too smart to make that kind of mistake? Consider this: poison oak changes appearance depending on whether it's in sun or shade—it can be a dense shrub or a climbing vine—so it's not always easy to identify. Even worse, the plant doesn't need its leaves to give you a rash: it has urushiol in its roots. If you're unlucky enough to come in contact with any part of poison oak, your only hope is to slather yourself in Tecnu, a special cleanser whose original purpose gives a sense of how insidious urushiol is—Tecnu was originally designed to remove radiation fallout dust from skin.

75 THE INSIDE OF A CHINESE COAL MINE

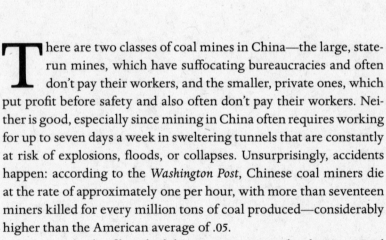

China

There are two classes of coal mines in China—the large, state-run mines, which have suffocating bureaucracies and often don't pay their workers, and the smaller, private ones, which put profit before safety and also often don't pay their workers. Neither is good, especially since mining in China often requires working for up to seven days a week in sweltering tunnels that are constantly at risk of explosions, floods, or collapses. Unsurprisingly, accidents happen: according to the *Washington Post*, Chinese coal miners die at the rate of approximately one per hour, with more than seventeen miners killed for every million tons of coal produced—considerably higher than the American average of .05.

As an example of how bad things can get, consider the No. 5 Coal Mine in Gangzi. On July 22, 2001, during the tenth hour of their shift, ninety-two miners died when gases ignited in a poorly ventilated shaft. Why was it poorly ventilated? Because it didn't have a ventilation system. Or, for that matter, a way to filter the coal dust from the air. It also had only one entrance, and its managers didn't routinely check for dangerous gases (mines in the United States do so every twenty minutes).

A banner outside of the No. 5 Coal Mine proclaimed that SAFETY IS HEAVEN—but it's unclear whether they meant that figuratively or literally. In either case, if you visit it or any of China's other mines, be sure to pack a canary.

THE SEATTLE GUM WALL

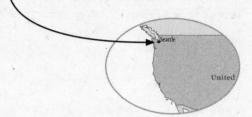

Upon finishing a piece of chewing gum, the polite thing to do is to throw it out; not toss it on the ground or stick it on the bottom of a chair, but find a garbage can. In extreme situations, it is acceptable to swallow. But under no circumstances should you be allowed to take the moist, warm wad out of your mouth, stick it on a public wall, and call it art.

Think I'm being too strict? Check out Seattle's gum wall. Tucked into an alley next to the Market Theater in Pike's Place, it's a brick wall covered with thousands upon thousands of wads of gum left there by people waiting in line. When the first masticated pieces arrived in the mid-1990s, the theater twice tried to remove them. But it was no use—the custom, as it were, stuck. The theater stopped fighting, and today, there are those who consider the wall an object of beauty.

I consider it disgusting. Some of the gum was originally used to affix coins to the wall—sort of a bastardized version of a wishing well—but this being Seattle, the money didn't last long. Now there's just gum, pounds of it, coating the wall in a layer so thick that in some places, you can no longer see any brick. There are sculptures of faces and dogs, initials surrounded by hearts, peace signs, and a multicolored American flag. One window drips with "gumsicles"; nearby, in a self-referential gesture, carefully shaped pieces of Wrigley's spell out GUM.

The wall's colorful, textured surface has made it popular with photographers. But even if you can't see it, the wall is hard to miss—covered in more than a decade's worth of Juicy Fruit, you can smell it from several feet away.

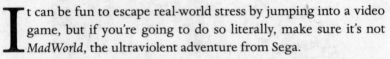

I t can be fun to escape real-world stress by jumping into a video game, but if you're going to do so literally, make sure it's not *MadWorld*, the ultraviolent adventure from Sega.

The game takes place in Varrigan City, a stylized, gritty dystopia where anyone you meet on the street is guaranteed to try to kill you. That's because three days before the game begins, Varrigan City was targeted by a terrorist group called the Organizers, who cut off the city's transportation and communication lines and unleashed a deadly virus that knocks out its victims in less than twenty-four hours after they catch it. The only way to survive is to kill another person—the Organizers promise a vaccine to anyone who commits murder.

In the true American spirit, the city's reaction to the outbreak is not to notify the CDC, but instead to transform Varrigan City into the set for a recurring game show called *Death Watch*, in which

---

* Not to be confused with Vatican City.

characters fight for the ultimate prize—their lives. Occasionally these matches are supplemented by special Blood Bath Challenges, where contestants complete tasks not usually associated with vacation travel, like knocking people onto a dartboard with a giant bat or trapping them in front of oncoming trains.

If you go, keep in mind that you'll be visiting as Jack Cayman, a character with a retractable chainsaw built into one arm. It's a lucky accessory, given the context, but be sure to use it wisely—players are awarded points not just for kills, but for style. "The amount of points for killing foes increases by increasing the foe's pain or using more unusual methods of killing," explains one description of the game. "For example, while the player could impale an enemy on a wall of spikes, the player will earn significantly more points if they had previously forced a tire around the enemy or stuffed the enemy in a garbage can before impaling him."

I know what you're thinking: how should I pack? In addition to a tourniquet and a machete, make sure you bring aspirin—the roughly sketched characters and streetscapes in Varrigan City are rendered in a headache-inducing palette of black and white that's only broken by the red of human blood.

78 THE INNER WORKINGS OF A RENDERING PLANT

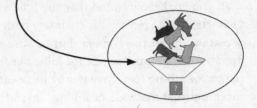

A s a kid, I used to eat dog treats. I didn't like the taste—I ate them because as an only child, gnawing on a Beggin' Strip gave me a sense of solidarity with the closest thing I had to a sibling: our family dog. But that was before I learned about rendering plants.

At its most basic, rendering is just a form of recycling. From slaughterhouse waste and expired meat to euthanized pets and deadstock, rendering plants take every type of nonhuman body part you can imagine and recycle it into protein, fat, and bone meal. Once isolated, these materials are used in everything from livestock feed to paints, lubricants, jet fuel, cosmetics, tires, and, yes, dog treats.

Gross though they may be, it's a good thing rendering plants exist: according to the National Renderers Association, America's rendering plants process about fifty-nine billion pounds of inedible animal by-products every year. If we didn't render, we'd be left with some pretty unsavory options: burying the carcasses (where they can leach into groundwater), incinerating them, or composting them (i.e., letting them rot).

None is as efficient as rendering, but that doesn't mean you want to visit a plant. Let's take the example of what happens to a dead cow. After being dragged into a truck and hauled to the rendering plant, it's put in a pile of other dead, bloated creatures, all covered in swarming maggots. A plant worker makes a small incision in its hide and inserts a tube that blows air between its skin and flesh, making it easier to remove the hide, which an employee then does by hand with a knife, being careful not to puncture the bloated gut. Once separated, the hide is preserved for leather, and the skinned carcass is ground into bits. This might very well be the most memorable sight from your visit: a dead, skinned beast, chain around its ankles, being jerkily lowered into a giant grinder like the dead body in *Fargo*'s infamous wood chipper scene. Brains, bones, organs, everything gets ground up in a roar, coming out the other end in a pulverized goo that's then boiled down to separate its ingredients.

Intrigued? You'll have to sign up for a tour. As for me, I'll never eat a Milk-Bone again.

79 AN AIRPLANE AFTER IT HAS BEEN STRANDED ON THE RUNWAY FOR EIGHT HOURS

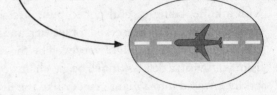

People's willingness to sit within inches of one another in a giant cigar tube with uncomfortable seats and stale air depends on a simple, but unbreakable, agreement: if you stay put and shut up, the plane will take you where you want to go.

So if something goes wrong and the plane can't take off—as was the case on December 29, 2006, with American Airlines Flight 1348 from San Francisco to Dallas/Fort Worth—airlines should take aggressive steps to avoid mutiny. In this particular case, strong storms in Dallas forced the plane to be rerouted to Austin, where American Airlines decided to keep it on the runway till the weather passed. Unfortunately, not only did the storms linger for hours, but they spread to Austin, making it impossible for the plane to take off.

In retrospect, American Airlines should have found a gate for the plane to park, or at the very least trucked food and water to the stranded passengers. But none of this happened. Instead, concerned about the hassle of rerouting an entire plane full of passengers during holiday season, American Airlines kept everyone on the plane. As time dragged on, flight attendants began running out of water; the only food on the flight, whose 6:05 A.M. scheduled departure was so early that many passengers hadn't eaten breakfast, was a box of pretzels. Despite the lack of beverage service, the plane's bathrooms began to overflow, and even after an airport worker emptied them five hours into the delay, the stench lingered throughout the cabin. Parents ran out of diapers for their children; one man exclaimed loudly that he had reached his last piece of Nicorette gum.

The plane languished on the runway for two, three, four hours. Finally, after eight hours of waiting, the captain, who admitted that he was "embarrassed" for American Airlines, made the executive decision to find a gate for the airplane himself. It took another hour for the plane to deboard. By the time the passengers got off, they had spent nearly fifteen hours on the plane—and still hadn't made it to Dallas.

80 THE AMSTERDAM SEXMUSEUM

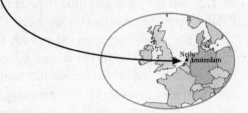

I t's hard to know how to react to museums dedicated to sex (specimens exist everywhere from New York to Prague). In theory, they seem like they should be titillating. But as is the case with the Amsterdam Sexmuseum, they're often less interesting than their subject matter would suggest.

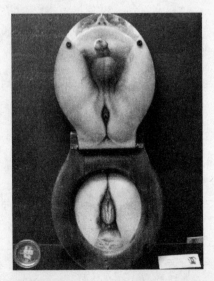

To its credit, the museum does have a fine selection of ancient stone dildos. But still, it's tough to fully explore sexuality in an institution whose most basic rule is that you should look, not touch. This is especially true in Amsterdam, a place where art and illicit intercourse happily coexist—the museum is just blocks away from De Wallen, Amsterdam's red-light district, which is helpfully indicated on museum maps. If you really want to see a twentieth-century wooden toilet seat painted with a bottom-up view of a dangling scrotum, then definitely stop by. But if you prefer a more hands-on approach to your education, there are other places in Amsterdam you might want to visit first.

81 THE NEXT ERUPTION OF THE YELLOWSTONE SUPERVOLCANO

Few things can put a damper on a family camping trip like the eruption of a supervolcano. So you might want to avoid being in Yellowstone National Park the next time it blows up.

It turns out that nearly all of the park's 2.2 million acres sit on what is one of the world's largest volcanoes—a volcano so massive that its full caldera is only visible from space. Its last major eruption was a thousand times as big as that of Mount St. Helens (the most violent eruption in modern American history) and emitted a plume of dust that spread over nineteen western states, plus parts of Mexico and Canada. As *National Geographic* describes it, "Dense, lethal fogs of ash, rocks, and gas, superheated to 1,470 degrees Fahrenheit . . . rolled across the landscape in towering gray clouds," which "filled entire valleys with hundreds of feet of material so hot and heavy that it welded itself like asphalt across the once verdant landscape."

These days, many of the park's attractions—its geysers, its hot springs, its bubbling mud pots—are made possible by the fact that the park sits on a giant magma chamber some forty-five miles across and up to eight miles thick. To give you a better sense of how massive this is, consider this quote from Bill Bryson's book *A Short History of Nearly Everything*: "Imagine a pile of TNT about the size of Rhode Island and reaching eight miles into the sky, to about the height of the highest cirrus clouds, and you have some idea of what visitors to Yellowstone are shuffling around on top of."

According to the Yellowstone Volcano Observatory, "If another large caldera-forming eruption were to occur at Yellowstone, its effects would be worldwide. Thick ash deposits would bury vast areas of the United States, and injection of huge volumes of volcanic gases into the atmosphere could drastically affect global climate." Luckily, they insist that there's no indication that a catastrophic eruption is imminent. But Bryson points to a different statistic: the supervolcano has erupted, on average, every 600,000 to 700,000 years. The last major eruption is estimated to have happened around 640,000 years ago. As Bryson puts it, "Yellowstone, it appears, is due."

Even if the supervolcano remains dormant, there's another threat: a giant earthquake. Yellowstone lies on a major fault line. In 1959, it was hit by a 7.5-magnitude quake that was so sudden that it caused an entire mountainside to collapse, sending some eighty million tons of rock hurtling off the mountain at more than one hundred miles per hour and killing twenty-eight campers.

82 THE SHORES OF BURUNDI'S LAKE TANGANYIKA WHEN GUSTAVE IS HUNGRY

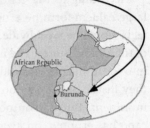

African Republic

Burundi

Gustave is not an irascible Frenchman; he's a giant crocodile in Burundi with a taste for human flesh. Thought to be more than sixty years old, Gustave is said by locals to have killed and eaten more than three hundred people.

This number is likely exaggerated, but scientists agree that unlike Bigfoot or the Loch Ness Monster, the huge croc actually does exist. Experts say it's quite possible he is twenty feet long and weighs around a ton—four times more than a typical crocodile. As one observer described him, Gustave has the girth of a killer whale and teeth the size of railroad spikes.

They also don't dispute the idea that he preys on humans. Corroborating reports from witnesses all describe a giant crocodile with the same distinctive dark scar on its head (thought to be an old bullet wound), and Patrice Faye, a researcher (and irascible Frenchman) who's been studying Burundi's crocodiles for more than twenty years, claims to have seen Gustave with people in his jaws. In 2004, he allegedly killed four swimmers in the span of eight days.

In addition to his stomach capacity, Gustave has impressive

powers of evasion. Faye has made several attempts to catch him, including one involving a massive, 32′ x 5′ x 7′ cage baited with a live goat, chickens, and, at one point, a sorcerer's unwanted dog. Gustave simply lingered in the river, his glowing eyes captured by nighttime cameras.

According to Faye's research, Gustave likes to alternate between an area of river in the Rusizi National Park and the banks of Lake Tanganyika, one of the world's largest freshwater lakes. When he eats, Gustave goes for quantity over quality, gobbling up easily detached body parts like heads, limbs, and abdomens and leaving the torsos behind. Satiated, he then retreats for up to months at a time. But don't be fooled by these temporary disappearances. Crocodiles have a neat trick where they can turn off their production of stomach acid and survive without new food for up to a year—just long enough for wary swimmers to let down their guard.

ANCIENT ROME ON OR
AROUND THE NIGHT OF
JULY 18, 64 A.D.

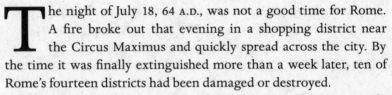

The night of July 18, 64 A.D., was not a good time for Rome. A fire broke out that evening in a shopping district near the Circus Maximus and quickly spread across the city. By the time it was finally extinguished more than a week later, ten of Rome's fourteen districts had been damaged or destroyed.

The causes of the Great Fire of Rome, as it was subsequently dubbed, remain mysterious. It could have been an accident—an estimated ten fires a day broke out in the city. The emperor, Nero, could have had the fire started to clear out a section of Rome where he wanted to build a new palace. Or, as Nero himself claimed, it could have been the Christians—there's evidence that Roman Christians of the time believed that Rome was destined to be destroyed by fire in 64 A.D., and someone could have just been trying to ensure that the prophecy came true. But then again, when it came to religious minorities, Nero wasn't the most reliable source: he liked to feed them to lions before gladiator matches.

Regardless of its causes, the fire had a lasting impact. Nero built the palace of his dreams, and the Circus Maximus, Rome's legendary chariot stadium, was completely redone. It remained open for races until sometime around 550 A.D., and besides casualties among charioteers (a frequent occurrence), the Circus steered clear of major catastrophe. Except, that is, for one day that's also worth avoiding: in 140 A.D., an upper tier of the balcony collapsed, killing more than one thousand people—sacrificial Christians not included.

84 NEVADA

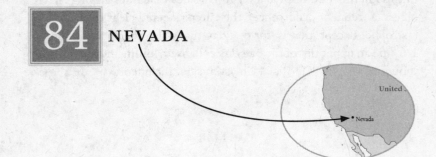

United

• Nevada

Dear 2.6 million residents of Nevada:

It's not my fault. When I asked friends and family to suggest places not to see before you die, six people independently insisted that I include the entire state of Nevada as an entry in the book. "But what about the salt flats?" I protested. "Or Red Rock Canyon? Or the Nevada State Mining Championships, held each year in Tonopah? There are good things in Nevada! And besides, people in Nevada buy travel books!"

But these friends didn't want to hear it. They wanted to talk about the heat, the emptiness, the atrocity that is Lake Las Vegas, the nuclear waste, the alien sightings, the fact Criss Angel calls it home. So for them, the Nevada haters, I am including this entry. Please forgive me.

A. The Vegas Strip

There are many, many things to dislike about the Las Vegas Strip, the main drag of Sin City that's known for its casinos, clubs, and, in the case of the Bellagio Hotel, a dancing fountain show set to "Luck Be a Lady Tonight." Complete with a fake Statue of Liberty, the Strip is also an example of Americans' willingness to accept reproductions of famous sights as adequate alternatives to the real thing. ("It's just like the one in New York City!" I heard a woman say, pointing at a replica of the Eiffel Tower.)

Some of the Strip's theme hotels are fun to walk around in, like the Venetian or Mandalay Bay. But most have no redeeming qualities. Consider the Luxor, a giant black pyramid guarded by an enormous sphinx. Despite having only opened in 1993, it has already managed to achieve an authentic feeling of decay, with dark hallways, faded faux-hieroglyphics, and unstable railings that provide only the slightest protection against falling hundreds of feet onto the casino floor below. The result is impressive, even for Vegas: a building that combines the despair of an existential crisis with the ambiance of a parking garage.

B. Nuclear Fallout

Nearly 80 percent of Nevada belongs to the federal government, which decided to take advantage of its vast deserts not for a drug-fueled art festival (see Burning Man, p. 217), but for nuclear explosions. Pockmarked with craters and larger than Rhode Island, the Nevada Test Site is the most notorious of the government's testing grounds. Between 1951 and 1992, it was home to more than one thousand nuclear detonations. While the tests' full fallout, if you will, remains unclear, in 1997 the National Cancer Institute concluded that atmospheric tests done in the area had contaminated large parts of the country with radioactive iodine–131 in quantities big enough to produce ten thousand to seventy-five thousand cases of thyroid cancer. I consider that reason enough not to visit. But others disagree—and for them, the U.S. Department of Energy has joined forces with NTS to offer free monthly tours.

C. Nuclear Garbage Dumps

When you do that much nuclear testing, you have to have some-place to put your garbage, and for a long time, the plan was to dump it at Yucca Mountain, conveniently located within the Nevada Test Site. Designed to hold more than seventy thousand tons of nuclear waste, the mountain seemed ideal: no one lives around it, its water table is deep, and besides, it's in a location *already* contaminated by nuclear waste. The federal government spent more than two decades—and billions of dollars—hollowing out the mountain in America's largest-ever public works project. Then in 2009, the project was scrapped. No one yet knows where America's homeless nuclear waste is going to end up (its eventual location will be another place not to visit), but in the meantime, there's at least one good reason to abandon Yucca Mountain: in 2007, geologists realized that part of the complex was situated directly on top of a fault line.

D. Aliens

Living in Nevada can make a person paranoid. If the government already used the state to test nuclear bombs, goes the logic, who's to say it's not up to other things? For example, concealing evi-dence of alien landings. Don't believe me? Go to Rachel, Nevada, a tiny town—or, rather, trailer park—some sixty miles from the nearest gas station on a road whose official nickname is the Ex-traterrestrial Highway. Tucked next to the mysterious Area 51 (a top-secret air force base), it's a mecca for some of America's most fervent believers in extraterrestrial life. And Rachel encourages them—its official Web site lists its population as "Humans 98, Aliens ??" and signs on telephone poles advertise an alien-sighting hotline. These days the town's main gathering place—and only business—is a motel called the Little A'Le'Inn, where visitors gather to swap stories of alien sightings over burgers and cups of coffee. It's worth a visit, but be careful—if you stick around long enough you have a high chance of being invited over to someone's house to watch home movies of UFOs.

The Sphinx at the Luxor Hotel (underneath is valet parking)

Fan Hours at the Las Vegas Porn Convention

There are some twenty-two thousand conventions in Las Vegas every year. Some are wondrous, many are boring, and a select few are terrifying.

You wouldn't, say, want to hang out with the guys from the military section of the surplus merchandise convention, as they tend to wear German helmets and play with stun guns. And very few people could be comfortable at the dentists' convention, which amounts to a room that's a couple hundred thousand square feet and filled with the maddened whine of drills, saturated by the smell of burning demonstration teeth, and sprinkled with giant screens showing gum tissue being abraded by lasers and pressurized water, melting like Nazis in *Raiders of the Lost Ark*.

But none of those compares to fan hours at the porn convention.

Technically, the AVN Adult Entertainment Expo is two shows. Downstairs, there's the business-to-business convention where porn shop owners browse the latest outfits, clamps, whips, gels, and miscellaneous toys in hopes of finding something new for their spring displays. This is initially titillating, eventually boring, and frequently confusing—as in "Really? A giant vibrating pink cone is the future of sex?"

Upstairs, though, is where you find the industry's personal side: the porn stars and their agents, directors, and many, many producers. Putting aside the clothes people are wearing, the videos that are being shown, and the fondling that often takes the place of handshaking, the atmosphere is pretty business-like. But woe unto you if you should be caught upstairs when the fans are let in.

The fans—they look like the crowd at a *Star Wars* convention after it's done time at a state institution. These are round and unshaven men, pierced and badly tattooed, many of them tumescent, all of them with cell phone cameras held high pressing against you, a scum-dappled tide lapping toward the performers. Like salmon who will never successfully spawn, they are single-minded and devoted in their quest, taking no notice of anyone trying to press through the crowd without touching them. Instead they bear you backward, grunting slightly. Up close you note their oily skin and an odor that suggests Axe has introduced its own line of nacho-flavored body spray.

When they reach the front of the scrum, they'll play it cool and casually tell the star how much they love her earlier work and that she showed great range in, say, the gang-bang scene in *Ass Trespassers IV*. She'll stand there in hot pants, with electrical tape over her nipples, smile a little distantly, and say, "Why, thank you."

Then each and every one of them will rest his head on her chest and smile as he takes a picture of himself, happy at last.

Interestingly, the massive Consumer Electronics Show and the porn show hit Vegas at the same time. The reason is that the porn show used to be part of CES (I'm not kidding). After all, the porn industry tends to be keenly interested in consumer electronics. Also, many CES attendees are keenly interested in porn.

BRENDAN BUHLER is a writer and staff reporter at the *Las Vegas Sun.*

✕✕✕✕

THE WORLD BOG SNORKELLING CHAMPIONSHIPS

United Kingdom

• Wales

Don't be scared if you see a snorkel tube rising from the murky depths of a bog while taking an otherwise relaxing walk in the Welsh countryside. You've likely stumbled upon a training session for the annual World Bog Snorkelling Championship, held each year in a specially designed course on a farm on the outskirts of Llanwrtyd Wells in Wales.

The site of the competition is quite scenic—it's even been designated as an area of "Special Scientific Interest" due to the rare and protected animals and plants that live nearby. But there is nothing pretty about the snorkeling competition. Originally started by the tourist board, it takes place in two sixty-yard trenches dug out of the peat bog. Protected animals and plants share space with hundreds of participants and spectators who gather on the banks to watch contestants race through the murky water, clad in everything from normal swimwear to wet suits to the occasional inflatable sumo wrestling costume.

As befits such a serious competition, there are, of course, strict rules: competitors are only allowed to compete in one of the two bog trenches, bog assignments are not transferable, and according to official guidelines, "No recognized swimming stroke may be used and lifting the head is allowed purely for orientation purposes."

If all that still leaves you wanting more, you're in luck: there's also a bog snorkeling triathlon.

D on't be that guy.

87 A NORTH KOREAN GULAG

N. Korea
S. Korea

The word "gulag" originally was an acronym for a Soviet bureaucratic institution called the Glavnoe upravlenie ispravitel'no-trudovykh lagerei—the Main Administration of Corrective Labor Camps. Like any Soviet bureaucratic institution, these original gulags were not fun places to visit—and while the word's definition has since expanded to include any forced labor camp, it still indicates a place that you don't want to experience firsthand.

North Korea provides some particularly good examples. Humanitarian groups condemn its "reeducation" camps for starving, torturing, and abusing prisoners, some of whom are there for crimes as small as listening to foreign radio shows. According to the *Wall Street Journal*, prisoners sometimes serve their entire sentences in the clothes they were wearing when they were seized—one woman had to bind her feet in rags after being arrested in high heels.

It's hard to imagine, but North Korea's *kwan li so* penal camps are reputably even worse than its labor camps. *Kwan li so* camps are home to North Korea's political prisoners, and are thought to hold somewhere between 150,000 and 200,000 people, some of whose so-called political offenses are as trivial as sitting on a newspaper containing a photograph of Kim Jong Il. Even worse, North Korea doles out punishments collectively, meaning that if one person in your family does something wrong, up to three generations of your entire extended family can be punished. The Hermit Kingdom is no doubt a fascinating place to see, but if you visit, make sure to play by its rules.

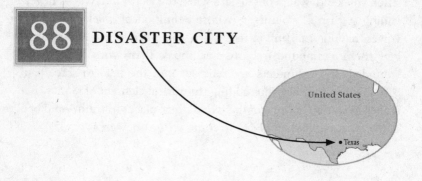

88 DISASTER CITY

United States

• Texas

S trolling through Disaster City on an otherwise pleasant Saturday, you're likely to be accosted by a bloody, screaming woman begging you to save her children from a collapsed strip mall or come across a pair of mangled feet sticking out from a pile of timber.

Don't worry—no one's actually been hurt. Disaster City is a fifty-two-acre urban search-and-rescue training ground at Texas A&M. Want to practice responding to an earthquake? Worried about a terrorist attack? Need practice searching for victims in an eleven-thousand-square-foot pile of concrete rubble? It's all here. A one-stop shop for simulated disaster, it comes complete with collapsed homes, a passenger train derailment, and a government complex inspired by the Oklahoma City bombing and built to replicate what might happen if a large explosion destroyed a three-story office building and parking garage.

As the largest and most comprehensive facility of its kind in the world, Disaster City is an invaluable training ground for rescue workers. Teams travel from around the globe to get a chance to practice here. But if you end up strolling through the city on a simulation weekend, watch out. That's when the victims arrive—a never-ending stream of volunteers whose definition of weekend fun involves having makeup artists burn their arms, cut their faces, give them compound fractures, or impale them with rebar. Once wounded, the volunteers are sent out into the field to scream in pain and beg for help, thus adding the critical element of reality that makes Disaster City one of the world's best places to train—and one of the most unpleasant places to come across unawares.

89 THE INSIDE OF A SPOTTED HYENA'S BIRTH CANAL

While most mammals maintain separate orifices for urination and giving birth, the spotted hyena makes no such accommodation. One of the most dominant predators on the African savanna, it does both through something called a pseudo-penis, a seven-inch fleshy protrusion that also happens to be its clitoris.

Considering that females also have fake scrotums and pseudo-testes, early researchers can be forgiven for being repeatedly confused when their "male" hyenas gave birth. But the title of this entry refers to what the inside of a hyena's birth canal would be like from the perspective of a cub. Imagine, if you will, trying to give birth to a two-pound hyena through your penis. Now imagine that you are the baby trying to get out.

GROPERS' NIGHT ON THE TOKYO SUBWAY

For a nonconfrontational person, I have some pretty aggressive daydreams. An example: when I'm standing on a crowded bus or subway, I like to imagine what I would do if a man tried to grab my butt. In my fantasy, I take hold of his hand and pull it into the air. "Whose hand is this?" I'd shout. "Was it yours? Because it was just on my *ass*." The offender would slink away in shame as my fellow passengers commended me for my wit and courage.

Suffice it to say, that has never happened.

But my chances might improve if I were to ride a crowded late-night train in Tokyo during *bōnenkai* season. *Bōnenkai* means "forget the year party" and is a December tradition similar to American office holiday parties: a professionally condoned excuse to get roaringly drunk. Unfortunately for female commuters, it also results in crowds of boozy men riding late-night commuter trains. Inhibitions unleashed, many of these gentlemen decide that there is no better way to ring in the new year than to grab a fellow commuter's bottom.

It's not just around the holidays, though. A survey conducted by the Tokyo metropolitan government and the country's largest railway operator found that 64 percent of women in their twenties and thirties reported being groped on public transportation. This became so much of a problem that in 2000, Tokyo's Keio Electric Railway Co. introduced female-only train cars.

Ladies-only cars make it easier to avoid having a stranger touch your boob, but they occasionally lead to a different problem: the assumption that any woman not traveling in the female carriage *wants* to be touched. Some critics say that instead of sequestering women, there should instead be groper cars, where like-minded men can congregate.

This would never really happen—what's the point of a groper commuting, after all, if he can't cop a feel? But perhaps some of them could be shunted off to an *imekura*, a brothel with rooms decorated to simulate public places. There are locker rooms filled with horny co-eds, doctors' offices staffed by naughty nurses, and classrooms full of skanky schoolgirls. And, now, subway cars—conveniently stocked with sexy commuters just waiting to be fondled.

91 THE YUCATÁN PENINSULA WHEN A GIANT ASTEROID HIT THE EARTH

Mexico

These days, Mexico's Yucatán Peninsula is a popular vacation destination better known for Cancun than it is for cataclysmic events. But if you happened to be hanging out on the beach near the town of Chicxulub sixty-five million years ago, the atmosphere wouldn't have been quite as relaxing.

That's when the Yucatán Peninsula got smacked by a giant asteroid; an asteroid so big, with such far-reaching consequences, that it may well have been what killed off the dinosaurs. Estimated to have been more than six miles in diameter, it slammed into earth at a speed of nearly twenty miles per second and left behind a crater about 110 miles across.

Scientists estimate that the force of the impact was some two million times more powerful than the largest nuclear bomb ever detonated. It sent megatsunamis crashing through the oceans, triggered earthquakes and volcanoes, and blasted up a storm of debris that became so hot when it reentered the atmosphere that it ignited wildfires around the world. Some scientists believe that the impact would have destroyed so many carbonate rocks—thus releasing a sudden giant spurt of carbon dioxide—that it would have caused an instant greenhouse effect. But even Al Gore would have had to ignore this prehistoric global warming to deal with a more pressing issue: researchers think the asteroid would have sent up a cloud of superheated ash dust so large that it could have covered the entire surface of the earth for up to a decade, blocking the sun, killing off many of the earth's species, and suggesting that sixty-five million years ago, you might have wanted to avoid visiting the earth at all.

92 MONDAY MORNING AT THE DMV

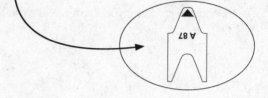

It's never fun to go to the Department of Motor Vehicles, the government bureaucracy better known as the tenth circle of hell or, and I really did hear this once, Satan's asshole.

That might be a little harsh. But regardless of which of Satan's orifices you decide to compare it to, there's no denying that much like the Dementors in *Harry Potter*, the DMV has a singular ability to suck people's will to live. And everything's worse on Monday, from the lines and crowds to the moods of the people who work there.

My favorite part of my local branch is that you have to wait in line to get a ticket telling you which line to wait in. But that's nothing compared to the experience of Laura Zhu, whose DMV disaster ended up on *AOL Money*:

> Newlywed Laura Zhu tried to get a license with her maiden name as her second middle name. When she explained this to the DMV worker at a New York City office, Zhu says the woman yelled at her, "You have to hyphenate if you want two last names!" After speaking with a supervisor and finding out that it is indeed

state policy to hyphenate, Zhu says she was sent back to the same window. That's when things got ugly. "Little Miss Doesn't-Want-to-Hyphenate wants a license now," the clerk announced loudly, then proceeded to sing a little tune as she worked: "Anderson hyphen Zhu! Anderson hyphen Zhu!"

It's enough to make you want to take the bus.

93 BLACK ROCK CITY

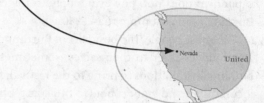

Black Rock City is the home of Burning Man, a giant art festival held each year in Nevada's Black Rock Desert. For devotees, Burning Man can be a life-changing experience, a chance to break free from societal norms and spend a week indulging in so-called "radical self-expression" in a giant, impromptu community. But if you don't enjoy being surrounded by drugs and naked people coated in glitter, you probably should not attend.

For starters, the festival is huge. The first Burning Man, held in 1986 on San Francisco's Baker Beach, drew twenty people. These days, it attracts around fifty thousand. To accommodate these revelers, every year Burning Man's organizers construct a temporary civilization—Black Rock City—on the desert's playa, an ancient lake bed. They set up a circular settlement centered around a giant anthropomorphic sculpture called "the Man" that is set on fire on the festival's last night and gives Burning Man its name. At the end of the weeklong party, the entire city disappears.

Burning Man's organizers provide emergency medical services and Port-O-Potties but that's about it—visitors have to bring everything they need to survive in the desert for a week. This is known as "radical self-reliance." To make things especially radical, no commerce is allowed in Black Rock City, and the only way to obtain things you don't already have is through "gifting," a Burning Man term for bartering with other partiers. This abhorrence of capitalism does not, however, apply to the entrance fee—tickets to Burning Man cost more than $350.

For most people, the best part of Burning Man is the art: burners, as attendees refer to themselves, sometimes spend the entire year building installations to bring to the festival, from refurbished steam locomotives and giant robots to full-size replicas of Victorian houses on wheels. But while it's amazing to see, for example, a large-scale stroboscopic zoetrope sitting in the middle of the Nevada desert, the experience is a little less fun when you're waiting in line for the communal toilet under the blistering midday sun.

That's the other thing about Black Rock City: its weather. During the day, thermometers regularly reach one hundred degrees; dehydration and heat exhaustion are common problems. But when the sun sets, the temperature can plummet fifty degrees, and it's not uncommon for predawn temperatures to approach freezing. Frequent wind storms send seventy-five-mile-per-hour gusts whipping across the desert, stirring up so much dust that festival organizers recommend packing masks and goggles to use during whiteouts. And then there's the dust itself. Highly alkaline, it can give you what's known as playa foot—a malady unique to the Black Rock Desert that is, in essence, a chemical burn.

Burning Man bills itself as being "radically inclusive," meaning that anyone and everyone is encouraged to attend (it's also "radically participatory," which tends to lead to a lot of drug use). This worked well when the festival was small, but now that Black Rock City's population is larger than most American towns, it's begun to experience some of the same problems as a regular metropolitan area, like bike theft, litter, sexual harassment, and even arson—during a lunar eclipse in 2007, several people were nearly killed when someone set fire to the Man five days ahead of time. (The accused suspect was the same man who, several years earlier, admitted to outfitting the sculpture with a giant pair of balls.) The Web site suggests not accepting open drinks from people you don't know, and warns that the area may be policed by undercover officers using night vision goggles to detect illegal drug trafficking, though the red eyes and vacant stares of many Burning Man participants suggest that this threat is not taken seriously.

There are also rules specific to Burning Man: "Do NOT burn other people's property!" says one. "Do not bring large public swimming pools or public showers," says another. And then there's my favorite: "Defecation on the playa is in violation of the law"—a regulation, it's worth noting, that wouldn't exist without good cause.

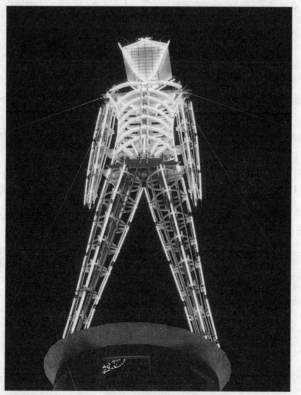

The Man

×××× **JENNIFER KAHN** ××××

Burning Man

The year I attended, there were a series of disasters, the most notable being when one of the Man's giant, mechanically-controlled arms got stuck mid-rise during the finale, with the result that it shot fireworks into the crowd rather than into the sky. That was also the year that a woman, presumably high, fell out of and was then fatally run over by her own Art Car.

There were dramatic events, but really, even without the bleeding and the screaming, the place is awful: a parched desert squat with the population density of a refugee camp, but with more noise—the ceaseless battering of amplified techno music—and less hygiene. I mostly hid in the bookmobile, where, on one particularly hot afternoon, a naked man offered me a filthy banana pancake, macerated after being clutched in his bare sweaty hand. Having been in actual refugee camps, I will say that Burning Man made those look like Tanglewood.

JENNIFER KAHN is a contributing editor to *Wired* magazine and contributor to *The Best American Science Writing 2009*.

××××

94 THE BOTTOM OF A PIG LAGOON

Vacations often take place around the water, so it's tempting to think that a pig lagoon might be a combination of two great things: a swimming hole and BLTs. In fact, what could be better?

If only. As the receptacle for all the waste generated by a modern pig farm, pig lagoons are filled not with water but with shit—and not just shit but everything else that falls through the grates of the pigs' cages. Blood, afterbirths, dead piglets—they all find their way into the lagoons, which, thanks to blood and bacterial interactions, are not brown but pink.

Lagoons can cover an area of up to 120,000 square feet and reach depths of about three stories. (The average pig produces three times as much feces as your average human, and we slaughter tens of million of pigs in the United States each year—you do the math.) The result is massive stagnant pools of waste contaminated with antibiotics, heavy metals, salmonella, giardia, cyanide, and everything else that passes through the pigs. Unlike most human waste, this sewage is never treated.

Occasionally the lagoons' polyethylene liners rip. If too much waste seeps under the liners and ferments, the ensuing gas pocket can rise up in the middle of the lagoon like a giant pimple, pushing pig sewage out into the surrounding land. Of course, the farmers are *already* putting it on the land—there's so much waste that a common way of reducing the lagoons' volumes is to spray the liquid onto fields as a fertilizer, or sometimes even to pump it directly into the air in hopes that some will evaporate. The resulting pig vapor contains gases like ammonia and hydrogen sulfide, and when inhaled can lead to bronchitis, asthma, nosebleeds, brain damage, seizures, and even death.

But inhalation is nothing compared to the ultimate risk—falling into a lagoon. Consider what happened when a worker in Michigan accidentally toppled in: "His fifteen-year-old nephew dived in to save him but was overcome, the worker's cousin went in to save the teenager but was overcome, the worker's older brother dived into save them but was overcome, and then the worker's father dived in," wrote Jeff Tietz in *Rolling Stone*. "They all died in pig shit." It's hard to think of a more horrible way to go.

95 SOHRA, INDIA, 10 A.M., DURING RAINY SEASON

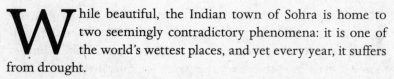

India

While beautiful, the Indian town of Sohra is home to two seemingly contradictory phenomena: it is one of the world's wettest places, and yet every year, it suffers from drought.

Located almost five thousand feet above sea level, it gets hit full force by the Bay of Bengal arm of the Indian Summer Monsoon, which drops an average of about 450 inches of rain per year, much of which falls during the morning. But thanks to Sohra's high elevation and deforestation, the water doesn't stick around—it runs off to the plains of Bangladesh, taking with it a healthy amount of soil and leaving Sohra's residents with a scarcity of potable water. Adding to the problem: the town has no reservoirs. Instead, when it rains, it pours—and when it stops, there's nothing safe to drink.

96 THE THING

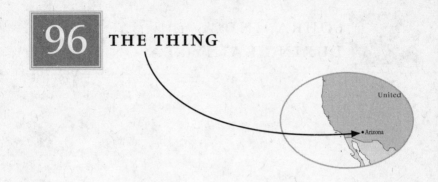

United

• Arizona

I will forgive you if, driving along Interstate 10 in Arizona, you stop to see the Thing. How could you not? Much like the Winchester Mystery House (see p. 20), billboards for the Thing—some 247 of them—advertise its existence for miles in each direction. MYSTERY OF THE DESERT, they tease. WHAT IS IT?

Whatever it is, it only costs a dollar—and besides, it's the only rest stop for miles.

But before you plan a family vacation around the Thing, let's clarify what you'll see. After you walk through a cave-like entrance in the gift shop, a path of yellow footprints leads you through two metal sheds, each filled with antiques and art of dubious quality and authenticity. In addition to a large caged display of wooden figures being tortured, the first shed is home to a car carrying several grumpy-looking plastic men. 1937 ROLLS-ROYCE, a yellow sign above it announces. THIS ANTIQUE CAR WAS BELIEVED TO HAVE BEEN USED BY ADOLF HITLER . . . *THE THING* IS, IT CAN'T BE PROVED.

The second shed is filled with objects of such supposed value that the designers of the Thing arranged them on scraps of polyester carpet in glass-faced plywood boxes. Among them: a so-called "ancient" churn dating all the way back to eighteenth-century Kentucky, an old grocery scale, and a sculpture of cows having sex.

Resist the urge to linger. The third shed is the home of the legendary Thing, housed in a white cinderblock box below a final yellow sign—and it'd be a bad idea to allow your excitement to build up for too long.

So what is it? An alien? A live dinosaur? No, my friends. The Thing is a desiccated mummy, holding another baby "thing" in its arms, its nether regions covered by an oversize hat. No further explanation is provided.

Believers point to the Thing's shriveled face and exposed rib as proof that it's a real mummy. But when the Phoenix National Public Radio station KJZZ did an investigation into its origins, it discovered that the Thing might actually be the work of a man named Homer Tate, a former miner and farmer who found a second career in creating props for sideshows. Using papier-mâché and dead animal parts, he spent his retirement crafting curiosities like devil babies and shrunken heads, which he advertised as "a wonderful window attraction to make your mother-in-law want to go home." Regardless of who's looking at it, the Thing is likely to have the same effect.

97 FOUR CORNERS

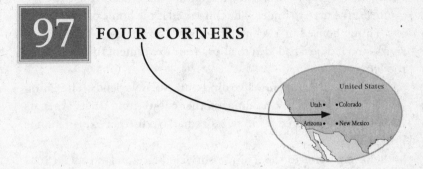

United States

Utah • • Colorado

Arizona • • New Mexico

here's something reassuring about the boxy shape of the states in the American West. It's as if surveyors got sick of dealing with the complicated borders of states like Maryland and just started drawing lines. The cleanest examples of this are the boundaries separating Utah, Colorado, Arizona, and New Mexico. Their straight, perpendicular borders meet at a spot called Four Corners, which is famous for being the only place where four states touch.

In 1912, this intersection was commemorated by a small cement pad. Clearly inadequate for such an important site, it was replaced in 1992 by a bronze disc embedded in granite. Emblazoned with each state's seal and bordered by the phrase FOUR STATES HERE MEET IN FREEDOM UNDER GOD, this new, larger plaque is much better suited for the main tourist activity at Four Corners: getting down on all fours so that you can take a picture of yourself with each limb in a different state.

If you go to Four Corners, make sure that you too engage in this geographic Twister. I say that because except for a small demonstration center where vendors hawk Native American jewelry and fry bread, there's not much else to do. As the Four Corners' PR department itself admits, "The area is very remote" and "The scenery immediately surrounding the Four Corners monument is somewhat bleak."

Adding to the confusion over why the monument counts as a tourist attraction: according to research by the National Geodetic Survey, it's actually in the wrong spot. In April 2009, the survey found that the Four Corners monument is a bit over 1,807 feet east of where it should be. Perhaps fearing the wrath of the tourists forced by parents and spouses to pose for embarrassing photographs in a spot now known to be meaningless, the NGS surveyors were quick to point out that since Four Corners has been *legally* recognized by all four states as the intersection of their borders, its current location, though inaccurate, is still legit. As Dave Doyle, chief geodetic surveyor for the NGS, told the Associated Press, "Where the marker is now is accepted. . . . Even if it's 10 miles off, once it's adopted by the states, which it has been, the numerical errors are irrelevant."

This existential approach to geography might help save the state the trouble of relocating the monument, but it also makes the entire experience seem a bit arbitrary. If any place can become Four Corners, why not just take a picture of your kid squatting on the intersection of a different set of perpendicular lines—like on a sidewalk—and visit Mesa Verde instead?

Russia

Okay, so prison isn't high on many travelers' life lists to begin with. But nonetheless, you should take special care never to land yourself in Russia's Prison No. OE-256/5, a hellhole otherwise known as Petak.

Like Alcatraz, Petak is on an island in a beautiful setting—in this case, Russia's White Lake. But unlike Alcatraz, it's still open for business. Petak is home to 170 or so of the country's most dangerous prisoners, and everything about it is designed to break their wills and destroy their spirits.

Prisoners are kept in cramped two-person cells for about twenty-two hours a day. For the rest of the time, they're allowed to pace back and forth in small outdoor cages—their only form of exercise. Prisoners are allowed two two-hour visits for the first *ten years* of their sentences. If they misbehave, they're put into a dark cell, empty except for a bucket and a fold-down bed, for fifteen days. Forget about books or entertainment—parcels are only allowed twice a year and, according to London's *Telegraph*, half the population has tuberculosis.

Anyone who tries to escape would either drown or be shot. But then, considering the effect Petak has on people, perhaps that's not a bad option. "After three or four years their personalities begin to deteriorate," the prison's psychologist told the *Telegraph* reporter. "There is no way anyone can spend twenty-five years in a place like this without being psychologically destroyed."

99 | A BIKRAM YOGA STUDIO

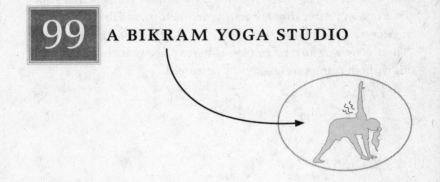

Walk into a Bikram studio—a branch of yoga that requires the room to be heated to 105 degrees at 40 percent humidity—and you'll be hit in the face with a steamy cloud of sweat and body odor so powerful that you'll be tempted to throw up.

Good thing there are sanitation standards for yoga studios, right? Wrong. There are none—a fact I'm reminded of every time I catch a whiff of Funky Door Yoga, a dog-friendly Bikram studio that, as all Bikram studios are *required* to do, carpeted its floor. That's bad news for my gag reflex, but it's great for the hundreds of thousands of bacteria that live in every yoga studio, sharing space on mats and blankets with dust mites, parasites, fungi, and viruses.

According to Philip M. Tierno, PhD, director of clinical microbiology at New York University Langone Medical Center, "Eighty percent of disease is caught by direct or indirect contact—either interacting with a person who carries germs or touching a surface where those organisms live." So let's see: you've got a moist, warm room populated by sickness-causing organisms that are spread by touch. Why bother with a yoga class? Just head to the hospital and lick some open wounds.

In addition to respiratory infections, things you can get from your downward-facing dog range from skin afflictions like athlete's foot, ringworm, and plantar warts to staphylococcus, a bacteria carried by more than 30 percent of people that can enter your body through a tiny cut or scratch and, if you're unlucky enough to get a drug-resistant strain, can kill you.

You can protect yourself by washing your hands, sanitizing your mat, and wearing a long-sleeved shirt, socks, and pants to class (everyone's outfit of choice when exercising in a rain forest). Or, alternatively, if you want an excuse to stay home from work, do Bikram in your bathing suit—an upsettingly common practice—and spend a few moments after class sloshing around on the floor. Somewhere in the sweat puddles is sure to lurk an organism that can give you a debilitating rash.

100 THE TRAVELING MUMMIES OF GUANAJUATO

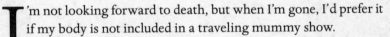

I'm not looking forward to death, but when I'm gone, I'd prefer it if my body is not included in a traveling mummy show.

That's exactly what happened to about 120 people who had the misfortune of being buried in a graveyard at Guanajuato, a town northwest of Mexico City. From 1865 till 1958, a local law required relatives to pay a grave tax for the privilege of keeping their kin underground. If you failed to pay the tax for three years in a row, your loved one would be exhumed, and his or her body—which was likely mummified, thanks to the area's arid climate—would be put on display in a museum.

I'm not kidding. The town is home to El Museo de las Momias—the Museum of the Mummies—and even though the grave tax law was changed in 1958, the bodies are still on display.

If you have a taste for the macabre, you might enjoy the exhibit. It includes a motley crew of human remains, from a tiny baby mummy who died (along with its mother) during a botched caesarian section to a woman whose raised arms and scratched forehead suggest that she might have been buried alive. Some of the mummies are clothed;

some are naked except for their socks. Beyond an occasional name, however, there's no information as to who they were or how they died.

I fall into the camp of people who think that maybe a traveling mummy show is not the most respectful way to deal with the remains of indigent Mexicans. But others disagree: the mummies are so popular that in the fall of 2009, they were taken to the United States for a seven-city tour.

By the second week of our honeymoon in Croatia, I knew that my husband, Peter, loved bell towers. Every time we found one, he insisted on climbing to the top so that he could take pictures from its panoramic view. So I wasn't surprised that when we arrived in Stari Grad—a small town on the island of Hvar—he made a beeline for the campanile.

But this bell tower was different. Unlike most Croatian campaniles, which are either padlocked or charge admission, it was unguarded, unlocked, and entirely covered in scaffolding. I am a cautious person and decided that a centuries-old building held up by a precarious network of wooden beams and metal bars might not be the safest structure to climb. By the time I'd reached that conclusion, however, Peter was already inside.

I entered to find him scampering up a set of steep stone steps, which were coated in a salt-and-pepper-colored layer of pigeon droppings so thick and crunchy that it sounded as if we were stepping on cornflakes. I took a few hesitant steps, asking spoilsport questions like "Do you think this is safe?" and "What if the building collapses?"

Paying no attention, he continued his ascent until the stone stair-case turned into several flights of metal stairs. In what had already become a theme in our relationship, I followed and soon found myself on a metal platform at the top of the tower, seven stories above ground. I was also standing directly beneath one of four giant metal bells, all covered in bird droppings and suspended just above head level. Peter, in the meantime, had leaped up onto the thick stone win-dowsill and was eyeing the wooden scaffolding outside—scaffolding of unknown quality, its age and structural integrity unclear.

"Come up here and take a picture with me," Peter said, gesturing toward the shaky wooden ledge. "It's got a great view."

At that point—the first moment all day—I refused. No, I would not come up on the windowsill. No, I did not want to take a picture. I was staying right here, on this shit-crusted metal floor beneath a huge bell, and if he thought I was going to let *him* jump onto the wooden scaffolding, subjecting me to the possibility of having to scrape my new husband's broken body off the concrete plaza below, he had another thing coming. No one was going *anywhere*.

Then I looked at my watch and noticed the time: 11:59 A.M. Quickly changing my mind, I decided I did, in fact, want to go somewhere—downstairs, to be exact, and fast. Barking a warning to Peter, I made a lunge for the stairs.

But I was too late. Before I reached the first step, I heard a click and a whir and looked up to see the bell directly above my head—six feet in diameter, with a clapper the size of a grapefruit—drop several inches. As the other three bells hung in silence, it shuddered slightly, paused just long enough for me to duck, and then sprang violently to life.

This was no slow, steady church bell. It was a frantic clanging, a call to arms, the sort of ringing you would expect if the town were about to be overrun by an intruding army or a giant tidal wave. I hunched over, hands clamped to my ears, as it rang and rang, send-ing crusted bits of bird poop cascading down on top of me and shak-ing the platform beneath my feet. Twenty times? Thirty times? I don't know how many times it rang; I only know that I was terrified,

sending desperate prayers for the floor not to collapse. Eventually
the bell clicked back into place and I brushed the droppings out of
my hair, grateful not to have been knocked unconscious or sent tumbling to my death. As my hearing slowly returned, I became aware of
a familiar, happy sound: Peter laughing.

✦ ACKNOWLEDGMENTS ✦

Many thanks to my agent, Rebecca Friedman, my editor, Allison Lorentzen, and the entire team at Harper Paperbacks that brought this book together, including Carrie Kania, Cal Morgan, Jennifer Hart, Stephanie Selah, Catherine Serpico, Michael Barrs, Greg Kubie, Alberto Rojas, and Amy Vreeland. Thanks as well to Sara Remington for her photography, Steven Korovesis for his illustrations, and the Gorlochs—Marcelino Alvarez, David Mikula, Shawn Bernard, and Adam Heathcott—for creating the 101 Worst Places app to expand the book beyond the printed page. I'm extremely grateful to my guest contributors and all the friends and strangers who submitted photographs, stories, and ideas—may your future travels be better than the ones described in this book. To my parents, grandmother, and Betty, thank you for instilling in me my love of travel, and for all the adventures we've shared. Lastly, thank you to Peter for your support, advice, and innumerable ideas—and for being the best partner I could ever hope for, in traveling and in life.

❖ PHOTO CREDITS ❖

✦ INDEX ✦

If you have additional submissions for the Web site, 101worstplaces.com, please send them to me at 101worstplaces@gmail.com.

Twitter handle: 101worstplaces

And join the Facebook fan page: 101 Places Not to See Before You Die

Get the app: 101 Worst Places